Frances Tenenbaum, Series Editor

HOUGHTON MIFFLIN COMPANY
Boston • New York   1997

Backyard Building Projects

Davidid Tenenbaum

Complete plans for more than 40 useful
or decorative objects to make for your garden

For Meg, my delight

Copyright © 1997 by Houghton Mifflin Company
Drawings © 1997 by Steve Buchanan

For information about permission to reproduce selections from this book,
write to Permissions, Houghton Mifflin Company, 215 Park Avenue South,
New York, New York 10003.

For information about this and other Houghton Mifflin trade
and reference books and multimedia products, visit The Bookstore at
Houghton Mifflin on the World Wide Web at http://www.hmco.com/trade/.

Taylor's Guide is a registered trademark of Houghton Mifflin Company.

Library of Congress Cataloging-in-Publication Data

Tenenbaum, David (David J.).
Garden building projects / David Tenenbaum.
    p. cm. — (Taylor's weekend gardening guides; 8)
Includes index.
ISBN 0-395-83812-6
1. Garden ornaments and furniture — Design and construction. 2. Animal
housing — Design and construction. 3. Plant containers — Design and construction.
4. Gardening — Equipment and supplies — Design and construction. 5. Garden
structures — Design and construction. I. Title. II. Series.
SB473.5.T45 1997
684.1′8 — dc21   97-22928

Printed in the United States of America

WCT 10 9 8 7 6 5 4 3 2 1

Book design by Deborah Fillion
Cover photograph © by Gay Bumgarner/Photo/Nats

CONTENTS

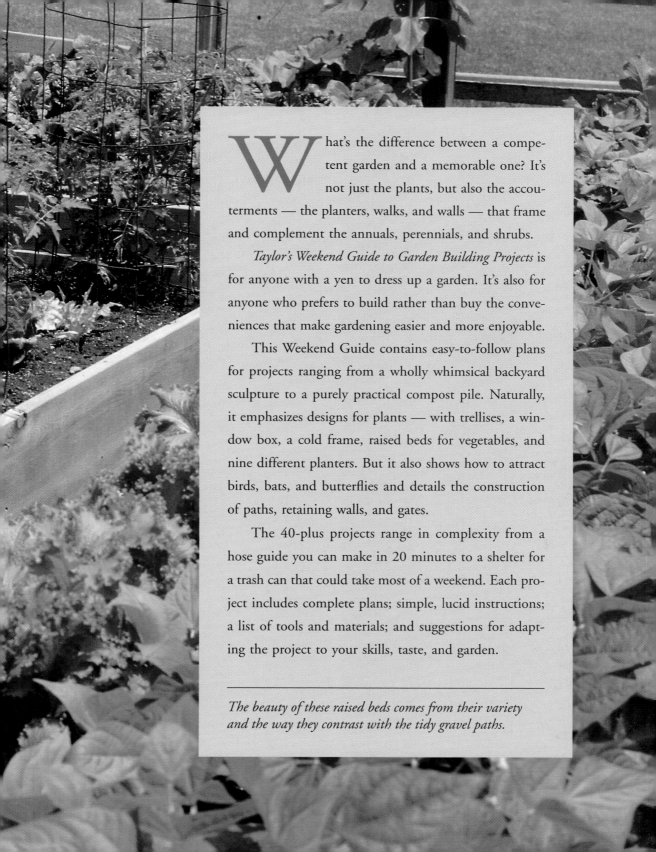

W hat's the difference between a competent garden and a memorable one? It's not just the plants, but also the accouterments — the planters, walks, and walls — that frame and complement the annuals, perennials, and shrubs.

Taylor's Weekend Guide to Garden Building Projects is for anyone with a yen to dress up a garden. It's also for anyone who prefers to build rather than buy the conveniences that make gardening easier and more enjoyable.

This Weekend Guide contains easy-to-follow plans for projects ranging from a wholly whimsical backyard sculpture to a purely practical compost pile. Naturally, it emphasizes designs for plants — with trellises, a window box, a cold frame, raised beds for vegetables, and nine different planters. But it also shows how to attract birds, bats, and butterflies and details the construction of paths, retaining walls, and gates.

The 40-plus projects range in complexity from a hose guide you can make in 20 minutes to a shelter for a trash can that could take most of a weekend. Each project includes complete plans; simple, lucid instructions; a list of tools and materials; and suggestions for adapting the project to your skills, taste, and garden.

The beauty of these raised beds comes from their variety and the way they contrast with the tidy gravel paths.

CHAPTER 1:
PLANTERS

Planters play a crucial role in many gardens, particularly smaller ones. Whether used on a deck, along a driveway, or in a narrow border between a building and a path, planters permit plants to occupy and beautify tight quarters. In formal settings, wooden planters help establish an architectural order in the garden. In informal settings, stone or hypertufa planters can complement a rock or cactus garden.

To use the first three wooden planters indoors, either line them with a waterproof liner or do your plantings in pots with saucers.

OBLONG WOOD PLANTERS (PLANTERS 1 AND 2)

This pair of wooden planters was designed for adaptability in size, shape, and embellishment. Planter 1, 31″ × 11″, is just 14″ high and can rest on bricks, a bench, or on legs you design. Planter 2, 17″ × 24″, has short legs and stands 22″ tall.

I suggest you decorate these planters with cutouts in the sides, made with a jigsaw or saber saw. For inspiration, use geometry, the sky, or your garden: diamonds, circles, stars, half-moons, fruits, and flowers all come to mind as patterns.

Tufa planters: Natural enough to fool most observers, you can make hypertufa planters in almost any shape.

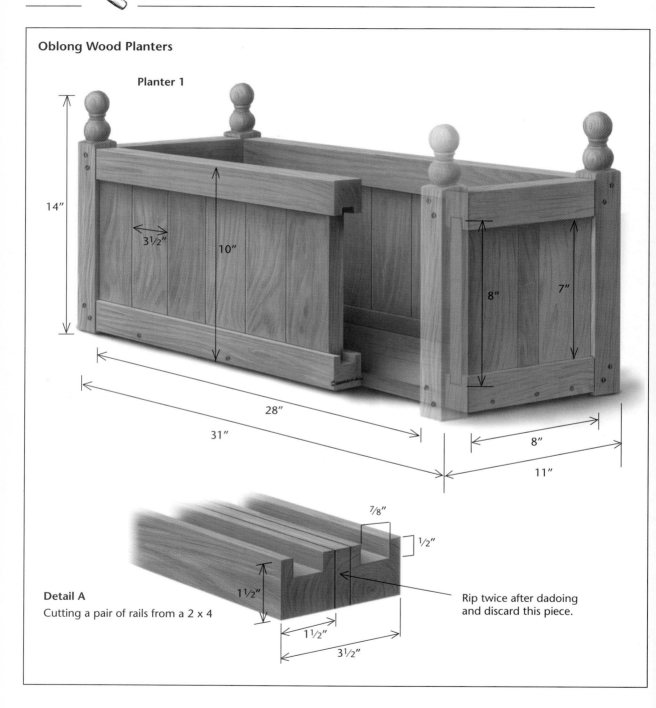

Oblong Wood Planters

Planter 1

14"

3½"

10"

8"

7"

28"

31"

8"

11"

7/8"

½"

1½"

1½"

3½"

Detail A
Cutting a pair of rails from a 2 x 4

Rip twice after dadoing and discard this piece.

I used a table saw and router for these planters, but if you're ambitious, you could get by with a circular saw and hand tools. You'll also need a variable-speed drill for fastening, and a jigsaw, coping saw, or saber saw to cut the decorations. It may help to have a power sander or rasp, and a countersink.

■ MATERIALS

Planter 1

One 7′ cedar 2 × 4

Two 8′ #3-grade cedar 1 × 4s

One 5′ pressure-treated 1 × 6

Two cedar railing spindles (at least 32″ long)

A handful of 3d, 6d, and 8d galvanized siding or box nails, and ³/₄″ roofing nails

Sixteen 2¹/₂″ rustproof deck screws

Sixteen 3″ deck screws

Two 1 ⁵/₈″ × 5″ truss plates

Planter 2

One 6′ cedar 2 × 4

One 12′ #3-grade cedar 1 × 4

One 6′ pressure-treated 1 × 6

Four cedar railing spindles

A handful of 3d, 6d, and 8d galvanized siding or box nails, and ³/₄″ roofing nails

Sixteen 2¹/₂″ rustproof deck screws

Sixteen 3″ deck screws

Two 1⁵/₈″ × 5″ truss plates

> **TIPS FOR SUCCESS**
>
> Most of the plans for wood projects in this book were written for the #3 cedar that's ⁷/₈″ thick. Before shopping, phone your lumber yard to ask if it sells this thickness in cedar. If you must use ³/₄″ thickness, adjust the plan dimensions accordingly. For more tips on using these plans, see page 113.

■ DIRECTIONS

Prepare the side rails

1. Planter 1: saw two 8″ and two 28″ 2 × 4s.
   Planter 2: saw two 14″ and two 21″ 2 × 4s.
2. Using a dado, circular saw, or router, saw two parallel, identical dadoes ⁵/₁₆″ in from each face of each 2 × 4. The dadoes should be ¹/₂″ deep × ⁷/₈″ wide, as shown in detail A on page 4.

Oblong Wood Planters

Planter 2

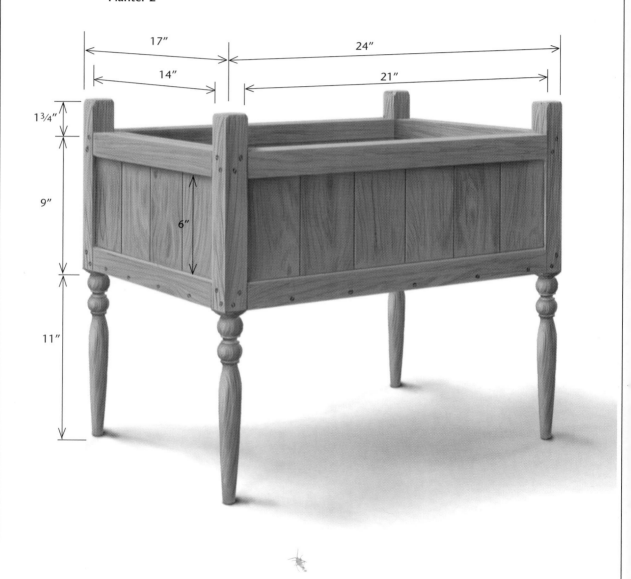

3. Rip these 2 × 4s twice to make four side rails and four end rails, each 1½″ wide.

Assemble the sides and ends

4. Crosscut the siding from 1 × 4:

    Planter 1: twenty-one 8″ pieces.

    Planter 2: twenty 7″ pieces.

5. Assemble one long side without nailing it.

6. Using drawing tools (or freehand if you've got talent!), draw a template for your decoration.

7. Trace the template design on the side boards, then remove them and carefully cut to the lines. Decorate more sides if you wish.

8. Reassemble the side, with all the good faces toward the eventual outside, and fasten with one 8d nail each at top and bottom. Take care that the nails don't come through the siding, and hold the side rectangular while nailing.

9. Fasten scrap lumber behind the cutout with 3d nails from the inside. This prevents soil from escaping.

10. Repeat step 8 for the second side.

11. Assemble each end as in step 8. For planter 1, rip two 1″ × 8″ pieces and place one of them between two 8″ 1 × 4s on each end.

Assemble the box

12. Planter 1: saw about 14″ from each end of two spindles to make four legs (discard the middle of each spindle). Round the spindle tops with a belt sander or rasp to make a fine-featured finial for each corner.

    Planter 2: saw four spindles to 21¾″ long, and discard the short piece. The square end goes up, and the shaped end makes the leg.

13. Hold a spindle in position at each end of each side, and countersink the two screw holes connecting it to the side rails. Fasten the spindle with two 3″ screws per joint.

14. Screw the spindles to the two ends to complete the box.

Finish up

15. Saw the bottom:

    Planter 1: two 28″ treated 1 × 6s

    Planter 2: three 21″ treated 1 × 6s

16. Rip these bottom boards as needed to fit flush with the bottom of the side rails.

17. Fasten the bottom boards through the side and end rails with 16 2½″ screws. Join the bottom boards on the inside with two truss plates. Fasten with ¾″ roofing nails driven at an angle so that they don't protrude through the bottom.

18. Drill a few ⅜″ holes for drainage in the bottom.

Tall Square Wood Planter

Since this 18″ × 18″ × 36½″ planter is relatively tall, it's built square for stability. You could easily build it closer to the ground if you wish. Please see the previous wooden planters for the tools you'll need.

■ **MATERIALS**

One 6′ cedar 2 × 4
Three 8′ #3-grade cedar 1 × 4s (see note page 5)
One 6′ #3-grade cedar 1 × 6
One 10′ #3-grade cedar 1 × 6
One 4′ pressure-treated 1 × 6
A handful of 3d, 6d, and 8d galvanized siding or box nails
Sixteen 2″ rustproof deck screws
Sixteen 2½″ deck screws

■ **DIRECTIONS**

Prepare the side rails

1. Saw four 17″ 2 × 4s.

2. Using a dado, circular saw, or router, saw two parallel, identical dadoes ⁵⁄₁₆″ in from each face of each 2 × 4. The dadoes should be ½″ deep × ⅞″ wide (see detail A of Oblong Wood Planters on page 4).

3. Rip these 2 × 4s twice to make eight identical side rails, each 1½″ × 1½″ × 17″.

Assemble the sides

4. Crosscut the side boards: 16 pieces of 1 × 4, each 15″ long. From 1 × 6, rip four more pieces 2⅛″ × 15″.

5. Assemble one side (without nailing), from four 1 × 4s, with one of the rippings from step 4 in the middle. Draw your decoration freehand or using drawing tools. Trace the design on the side boards, remove them, and carefully cut the patterns. Decorate more sides if you want.

6. Reassemble the side, keeping it rectangular. Fasten each board with one 8d nail each at top and bottom, with all good faces to the eventual outside. Don't nail near the ends of the side rails, since you'll be beveling them in step 9.

7. Place scrap lumber behind the cutout, and fasten with 3d nails from the inside. The scrap covers the hole and holds soil in place.

8. Repeat step 6 on three more sides. (The sides are identical, except for any decoration.)

9. Bevel both ends of each side assembly at 45°, taking care to avoid sawing into nails. Note: The angle is on the inside face, and the overall width is 16¹⁄₄″ after beveling.

Assemble the box

10. Assemble the four sides by countersinking and screwing through the mitered ends of the side rails with 2¹⁄₂″ screws. Check that the box remains square as you work.

11. Saw the bottom from three 13¹⁄₂″ treated 1 × 6s. Rip as needed so that the boards fit inside the box, resting on the top of the lower side rails.

12. Position these bottom boards and fasten with a few 6d nails driven diagonally into the side rails.

13. Drill four ³⁄₈″ holes in the bottom for drainage.

Make the legs

14. Saw four 1 × 6s to 35⁷⁄₈″. Then rip to 4³⁄₄″.

15. Saw eight leg pieces from these rippings as shown in detail B on page 11. Note: Mark, number, and saw two boards (four leg pieces) with the good face up. Repeat with the good face down to make another four pieces.

16. Optional: With the saw set to cut ¹⁄₄″ deep, saw two parallel kerfs as shown to decorate all four wider legs.

17. Before nailing, hold the legs against the assembled planter, at the locations indicated. If the leg tops are not flush to the planter top, recheck their posi-

Tall Square Wood Planter

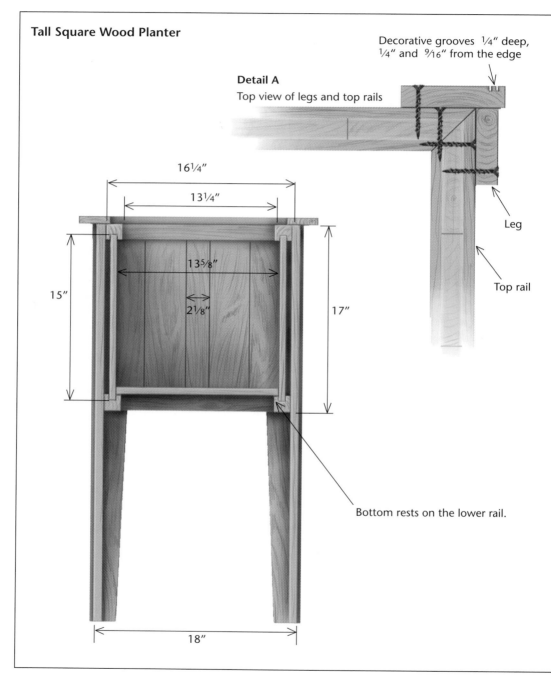

Decorative grooves ¼" deep, ¼" and ⁹⁄₁₆" from the edge

Detail A
Top view of legs and top rails

16¼"

13¼"

13⅝"

2⅛"

15"

17"

18"

Leg

Top rail

Bottom rests on the lower rail.

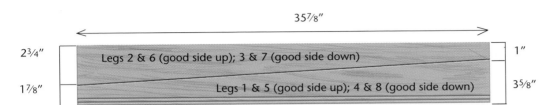

35⁷/₈"

2³/₄"

Legs 2 & 6 (good side up); 3 & 7 (good side down)

1"

1⁷/₈"

Legs 1 & 5 (good side up); 4 & 8 (good side down)

3⁵/₈"

Detail B
Cutting the leg pieces

Leg numbering

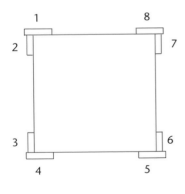

tion with the leg numbers. Nail pairs of leg pieces together, with the good side out and a $1/4''$ overhang.

18. Screw each leg assembly to the side rails with four $2''$ screws, with the leg tops flush to the planter top.

19. Saw four trim pieces, $1/2'' \times 2''$ by $20''$ long from the remaining 1×6. (If you don't have a table saw, don't bother ripping to $1/2''$ — just use the $7/8''$ thickness.)

20. Miter both ends to make two of these pieces $1''$ longer than the width, and two $1''$ longer than the length. (Since you're measuring from the corners of the legs, width does not equal length.) With two 8d nails, fasten these strips to the legs, making sure they overhang equally.

HANGING PLANTER

You can use this design to hold a $6''$ round pot or to hold soil inside sphagnum moss. If you've got a tall pot, don't hesitate to add a layer or two of extra rippings to the top of this design. In fact, you can use this log-cabin technique to make a much larger planter too, once you get the hang of it. Think of it as kid stuff — playing with logs.

The entire planter is made from $7/8'' \times 7/8''$ rippings, sandpapered, with the good face out. When you're done, you could suspend the planter from a tree or an eave, although I found that it also looks good in the living room. For making this planter, it would be helpful to have a table saw or circular saw, and a drill with countersink.

■ MATERIALS

One $4'$ #3-grade cedar 1×6 (see note page 5). Make sure the piece is not too knotty.

Thirty-six $15/8''$ deck screws

Four $11/2''$ galvanized screw eyes

One $21/2''$ galvanized screw hook

$10'$ galvanized wire

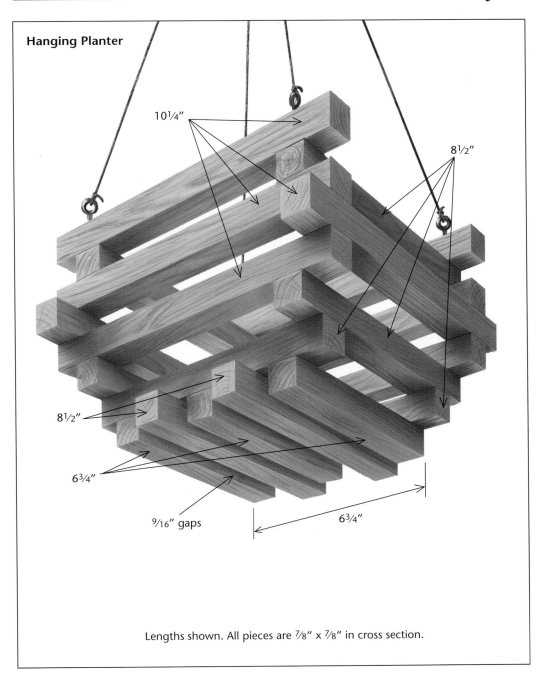

Hanging Planter

10¼"

8½"

8½"

6¾"

⁹⁄₁₆" gaps

6¾"

Lengths shown. All pieces are ⅞" x ⅞" in cross section.

■ **DIRECTIONS**

1. Rip five pieces of cedar to $7/8'' \times 7/8'' \times 48''$.
2. Saw layer 1: two $81/2''$ pieces and three $63/4''$ pieces.
3. Saw layer 2: two $81/2''$ pieces.
4. Using a square to get the 90° angles, alternate the shorter and longer pieces in layer 1, and screw layer 2 to layer 1. Make a shallow countersink at each corner (if you go too deep, the screw tip will protrude), and drive a screw at each joint.
5. Cut two pieces each to these lengths for the subsequent layers:

   Layer 3: $81/2''$

         4:     $101/4''$

         5:     $101/4''$

         6:     $101/4''$

         7:      $81/2''$

         8:     $101/4''$

6. Fasten each layer either flush to the preceding layer, or with a $7/8''$ relief. If the joint is directly above a screw, drill at an angle so that you miss it.
7. Drill and insert a screw eye at each corner.
8. Fold the wire in half, and cut it into two equal pieces. Bend the two wires in half again, and use a locking pliers to twist a loop at the center.
9. Loop the ends through the screw eyes so that the planter hangs level.
10. To hang the planter from the eaves, screw the screw hook into framing wood.

LOG PLANTER

If you can get your hands on a portable-sized weathered log, it's pretty simple to Paul-Bunyan it into shape, particularly if a friendly friend has a chain saw.

Saw the log lengthwise, leaving enough to make whatever depth of planter you desire. The hard part is hollowing out the log. I'd use a $1''$ or $11/2''$ auger bit in the biggest electric drill I could get my hands on (it might make sense to rent a $1/2''$ drill or a wonderful tool called a "hole saw" for a few hours).

Wrap masking tape around the bit so that you don't wind up drilling through the other side (the "China syndrome"). Then mark the area you want to remove, and make as many holes as possible in the inside. Finally, with a hammer and big chisel, remove the broken-up wood, and smooth the insides as much as you think necessary. Don't go overboard with the smoothing work — I don't think plants get splinters in their roots.

LANDSCAPE TIMBER PLANTER

Here's the word on railroad ties: they make great planters — if you can afford back surgery afterwards and if you crave the lingering stench of carcinogenic creosote in the garden. Fortunately, there's a better alternative: landscape timbers. These 8′ timbers are $3^1/_2'' \times 5''$ wide, with two $3^1/_2''$ faces rounded off. They're cheap, much lighter than railroad ties, easy to work, and are impregnated with nonstinky preservative. In fact, they're as handy for raised beds as they are for planters.

Building a planter with timbers couldn't be much simpler. Lay out the area and tamp the soil. Build up the planter log-cabin style, using overlapping joints. Use two 6″ to 8″ polebarn nails per joint — one horizontal, and one vertical.

Landscape Timber Planter

Stone planter: A dry stone wall makes a good planter, helping you convert a plain stucco wall from a liability into an asset.

Hammer another nail about every 3′ to 4′ along the straight lengths. Use from one to four layers of timbers. If you have trouble driving the nails, drill partway through the top timber first. Tip: Drive these spikes with a John-Henry-size hammer, say, a three-pounder.

STONE AND BRICK PLANTERS

Stone and brick make great planters, particularly if you want to complement paths made of similar materials (we'll get to paths later on). Like politics, all stone is local, so it's hard to generalize about what you'll find. Look for a variety that's comely, stackable, and fairly regular in size. Bricks must be the high-fire variety, since low-fire bricks absorb water and don't resist freeze-thaw degradation. To test whether a brick was high-fired, dunk it briefly in water, and notice how quickly it absorbs the water. If the surface dries out within half a minute or so, the brick was not high-fired and is unsuitable for ground contact.

If you want to mortar the masonry, you will need to go to great lengths to prevent cracking by placing footings below the frost line and figuring out how to keep the soil in the planter from expanding in winter. I'd go to the other extreme and build flexibility into the planter by skipping mortar entirely and staying close to the ground — say 12″ to 15″ maximum.

Laying mortarless "dry" bricks is a no-brainer, and stones are only slightly more complicated. Start by marking the perimeter with string. Set the stones flatter-side-down, in a position where they rest naturally. You may have to chink the holes by placing smaller stones inside so that soil does not leach out. You may also have to restore the bricks or stones to position after a hard winter. For more on building with stones and bricks, see Retaining Walls, page 76.

FLUE TILE PLANTER

Clay flue tile, sold by masonry suppliers, makes an easy, cheap, and attractive planter, especially if you group several of them. Flue tiles are made in 24″ lengths. Round flue is sold with inside diameters ranging from 6″ to 18″. Rectangular tile starts with an inside measurement of 8″ square, up to a back-breaking 18″ × 24″.

Before you start thinking this stuff is the ultimate answer to planters, remember that large flue is extremely heavy. And although terra cotta is attractive, it's not terribly strong, so flue tile is probably best suited to areas with warm and/or dry winters. In colder climates, you can reduce the chance of tiles cracking in the winter by putting plenty of gravel at the base for drainage. It might be a good idea to cover the planter in fall to keep rain and snow out.

You can cut tile with a masonry blade on a circular saw. Carefully mark your line with a crayon, and put on a dust mask and goggles. Then saw carefully, with the flue well supported so that it doesn't crack or bind the saw. It's smartest to use several shallow passes to complete the cut. (If you're eager to shirk the nasty job of cutting flue — and nasty it is — you may be able to pay a brickyard to make the cuts.) Finally, place the cut end down, since it's more homely than the factory end.

HYPERTUFA PLANTER TROUGHS

Looking for a rough-textured outdoor container that complements a rock or cactus garden? Your answer may be an organic-masonry planter made of tufa. Tufa, AKA hypertufa, is a cheap, versatile material made of equal parts perlite, sphagnum peat moss, and dry Portland cement. A trough 15″ square calls for about 3 gallons of mix.

The stuff is held together with a handful of "Fibermesh" reinforcement material in each gallon of mix. (To find a Fibermesh dealer, contact Fibermesh Company, 4019 Industry Dr., Chattanooga, TN 37416; 423-892-7243.) You can color the "stone" with an ounce of powdered cement color (available at a masonry supply house) per gallon of mix. Be sure to read the toxicity warning on the coloring.

Make the Molds

You can improvise molds from plastic household tubs, wood, or used plant containers. Because sharp corners are easily chipped, your mold needs rounded corners. Two rectangular tubs, one 4″ longer and wider than the other, will nest together to form a trough with sides 2″ thick. Make a round container by nesting a 7-gallon plastic nursery container inside a 10-gallon container, leaving about a 2″ gap for the tufa. Coat the contact surfaces before each use with linseed oil to prevent sticking.

If your mix is stiff enough, you can skip the inside mold. Damp sand covered with plastic will even work if you pay special attention to avoiding weak spots and sharp corners.

Mix the Mix

Once the mold is ready, mix the dry ingredients to the proportions above, in a wheelbarrow or large bucket, or on a scrap of plywood. A hoe or shovel will work equally well for mixing. Protect your hands with rubber gloves and your lungs with a dust mask. When the dry ingredients are thoroughly mixed, add just enough water to produce a muck the consistency of cottage cheese. Remember: we're not making stone soup here!

Forming

Cover a worktable with a plastic sheet, and position the outer mold on it. Then, with gloved hands, pour the mixture until the trough bottom is 2″ thick. Place the inner mold in position, and push down to pack the tufa. Leave the inner mold in place, and pack tufa tightly between the molds. Wait 10 minutes and remove the inner mold. Form drainage holes in the bottom with a 1/2″ dowel, and round off the inner corners if needed. Don't move the mold, and cover it with plastic so that it doesn't dry too quickly, which would weaken it.

Making a Hypertufa Trough

1. Pack the tufa mix into the bottom of the outer mold about 2" thick, and work the mix partway up the sides.

2. Insert the inner mold, and continue to pack tufa between the molds.

3. After about 10 minutes, carefully remove the inner mold and form drainage holes with a $\frac{1}{2}$" wooden dowel.

4. Brush the outer surfaces of the cured trough with a wire brush; carefully burn off "hair" on the surface with a propane torch.

Curing

After the container has cured 48 hours, remove the outer mold, and brush the outside with a wire brush to improve the texture. Don't worry if this creates a "cat hair" look — you'll burn off the hairs later on. Without moving the trough, replace the plastic cover and allow another two weeks of curing.

Now you can move the trough, but delicately, to avoid hairline cracks. Wash the trough several times with water as it cures to leach out the lime, which would otherwise raise the pH of your potting soil.

After two more weeks, burn off the cat hair with a propane torch. Keep the torch moving to avoid heating one spot too much — damp pockets in the walls might burst and cause pits or cracks. (Thanks to Ernie Whitford, an avid Colorado rock gardener, for these directions.)

To plant, cover drainage holes with crockery or wire screen, then add soil mix. To make a natural-looking rock garden, sink rocks halfway in the soil. Dig your planting holes, plant, and cover the surface with gravel (available at an aquarium store) that matches the rocks. To overwinter your plants in a cold climate, place them in the shade or in a cold frame. Either step should prevent freeze-thaw cycles from harming the plants or the trough.

WINDOW BOX

What could be simpler or more satisfying than building a window box? Then build a pair of them for the windows that flank your overly plain entryway or look out on an asphalt-contractor's-dream driveway. As far as decoration is concerned, you can appliqué wood to the box, find decorative finials, or jigsaw the face, as described previously for wooden planters. For our Shaker-sympathetic readers, I've left the box plain, strong, and (I hope) of graceful proportions.

This design is 32″ × 12″ deep (at the front) × 10 1/4″ high. To adapt it to different width windows, simply alter the length of the back beam (it's 1 3/4″ shorter than the overall width). Although the frame is slightly complicated (to make the box strong but not ponderous), once the frame is made, you can just mark the sheathing boards by placing them in position on the frame.

I used a table saw, mainly because I have one, but you could get away with a circular saw and regular hand tools. You'll also need a variable-speed drill for screwing, and a countersink.

Window Box

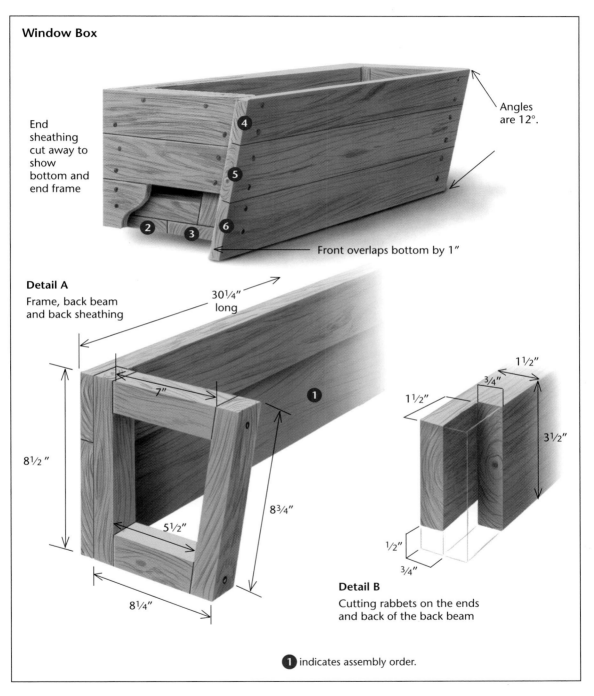

Angles are 12°.

End sheathing cut away to show bottom and end frame

Front overlaps bottom by 1"

Detail A

Frame, back beam and back sheathing

30¼" long

8½"

7"

8¾"

5½"

8¼"

Detail B

Cutting rabbets on the ends and back of the back beam

1½"

1½"

¾"

3½"

½"

¾"

1 indicates assembly order.

■ MATERIALS

One 6′ pressure-treated 2 × 4

One 8′ pressure-treated 1 × 6

One 6′ #3-grade cedar 1 × 4 (see note page 5)

A handful of 6d and 8d galvanized box nails

Rust-resistant deck screws: approximately twelve 1⅝″and twelve 3″

Two ⁵⁄₁₆″ × 3″ lag bolts and flat washers for mounting

■ DIRECTIONS

Make the end frames and back beam

1. Rip a 36″ 2 × 4 twice, making two pieces 1½″ × 1½″.

2. From these pieces, saw two sets of top, bottom, front, and back rails for the end frame, using dimensions from the drawing. Make the angle (miter) cuts at 12°.

3. Countersink and fasten the end frames using one 3″ screw per joint (see detail A on page 21).

4. Using a table saw, circular saw, or router, saw a rabbet ½″ tall × ¾″ deep all along the bottom rear of a 30¼″ piece of treated 2 × 4. This is the back beam (see detail B on page 21).

5. Cut ¾″ × 1½″ rabbets on the front face of both ends of the back beam (see detail B on page 21).

6. Fasten the end frames to these rabbets with two 3″ screws.

Sheath the back and bottom

7. Saw three pieces of pressure-treated 1 × 6, 30¼″ long for the back and bottom sheathing. See drawing for the sheathing order.

8. Slip board #1 into the long rabbet on the back beam, a) resting against the end frames and b) flush to the bottom and ends of the end frames. Screw board #1 to the end frames with two 1⅝″ screws per end.

9. Lay board #2 into position. Mark board #3 and bevel its front edge flush with the front of the end frames. Fasten both with 1⅝″ screws.

Sheath the front and ends

10. Cut three pieces of cedar 1 × 4 to 33¾″ for the front.

11. Bevel board #4 at 12°, and nail it into position with the beveled top flush

with the top of the end frames. Board #4 overhangs the end of each end frame by $1\frac{3}{4}''$.

12. Nail board #5 into place.

13. Mark board #6 at 1″ below the bottom sheathing, then bevel to the mark at 12° so that the bottom edge is horizontal. Nail into place.

14. Cut 12° miters on one end of six pieces of 1 × 4 that are at least 11″ long.

15. Hold these pieces in position on the ends. The top board is flush with the top of the end frame. The bottom of the bottom board is flush with the bottom of the front sheathing. Mark the backs along the back of the rear sheathing, cut to size, and nail.

Finish up

16. Drill six $\frac{3}{8}''$ holes in the bottom for drainage.

17. Drill two $\frac{1}{4}''$ holes in the back beam for lag screws to fasten to the house framing.

18. Place the window box against the windowsill, and lag-screw into the framing. You may need to shim the back so that the box sits level.

RAISED BEDS

Raised beds have boosted the standard of vegetable gardening considerably around my micro-farm by preventing soil compaction, allowing the soil to warm up quickly, and giving the whole thing a spic-and-span air that helps distract the eye from summer's inevitable invasion of weeds. Since raised beds made of stone or brick are really just planters, I'd suggest adapting our plans for stone and brick planters. In the garden we call Joshie's Jungle, we made raised beds from landscape timbers. To do that, adapt the material on page 15.

For raised beds made from lumber, I'd consider using CCA (copper-chromium-arsenic) pressure-treated wood, since little of the preservative chemical seems to leach out. If you can, look for an equivalent material that omits arsenic from the recipe. The problem with untreated wood, obviously, is that you'll have to replace the edging more frequently. It's standard to warn against using wood treated with creosote or pentachlorophenol, but wood containing those toxic chemicals is off the market.

Raised Beds

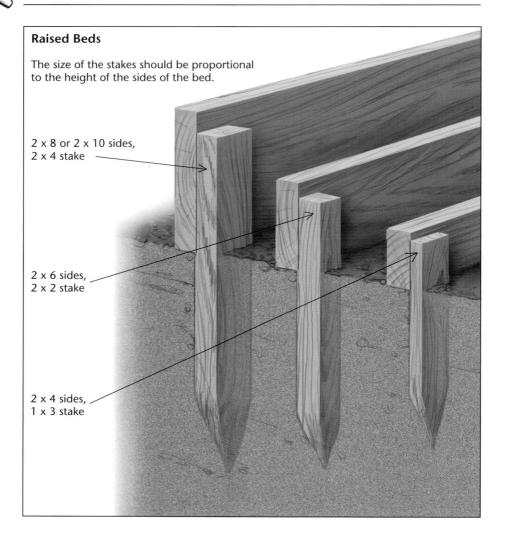

The size of the stakes should be proportional to the height of the sides of the bed.

2 x 8 or 2 x 10 sides, 2 x 4 stake

2 x 6 sides, 2 x 2 stake

2 x 4 sides, 1 x 3 stake

In general, the beds should be no more than 5′ wide so that you can reach to the middle. Pathways should be 16″ to 24″ wide, just enough for you to walk and work in. If you plan on hauling much compost into the garden, make relatively wide pathways so that you can maneuver a wheelbarrow. And do profit from my mistake: put the stakes on the bed side of the boards so that they won't snag your wheelbarrow. The size of wood and stakes, as you'll see in the drawings, depends on how high you want the beds.

Raised beds: *The beauty of these raised beds comes from their variety and the way they contrast with the tidy gravel paths.*

Here's the basic technique for making wooden raised beds:

1. Lay out the beds with string and stakes.
2. Scoop some soil out of the path areas to deepen them about 2″, and throw it into the bed areas.
3. Pound the corner stakes into place (always sharpen wooden stakes with a saw or hatchet — otherwise, they will split).
4. Use galvanized nails to nail the boards to the stakes. Try my old friend John Christenson's favorite trick for hammering to a moving target: hold a second hammer behind the stake to absorb the shock and ensure a tight fit. Or use rustproof deck screws, which are stronger and easier to drive.
5. Drive stakes about every 3′ along straight sections.
6. When done, fill the bed to about 2″ from the top, allowing room to add soil amendments.

CHAPTER 2:
PLANT HELPERS

I f your garden is good enough, visitors will see only what you intend them to see — the plants and the planters and ornaments. What they won't see is the infrastructure that makes your garden the verdant place it is. But as any gardener knows, gardening is not just about sticking plants into the ground, but also about making compost, mixing and straining soil, raising seedlings, and supporting delicate plants in their search for sun and air.

COMPOST BINS

Compost — what garden can live without its life-giving, humus-enhancing benefits? When I was growing up, Mom used to dump the leaves I so arduously raked into a corner behind the garage. Then I got to play "fort" in the pile while it decomposed. But that live-and-let-rot technique is neither the fastest nor the most efficient way to get from "point melon rind" to "point humus."

Instead, make yourself a pair of compost bins — one for starting the decomposition, and the second for completing it. Make the bins porous enough to allow oxygen to reach the heap. Make them big enough so that they have a warm, insulated interior where bacteria and fungi can really get cooking for hyper-speed decomposition. And, for the same reason, try to locate the bins in the sun.

Trellis: *This simple trellis is great for keeping cucumbers, squashes, and tomatoes off the ground.*

I've designed a heap as a pair of 3′ cubes; naturally, you can vary the size to suit your own preferences about rot and decay. To make these bins, I would beg, borrow, or rent a post-hole digger to make holes for the corner posts. You'll also want a carpenter's square and a level. If you're nervous about the possible migration of toxic chemicals from pressure-treated lumber into your compost, you can use untreated wood throughout, but this will considerably shorten the life of your heap. I compromised by making the posts of CCA-treated lumber, and the sides, which have more contact with the compost, of untreated cedar. That way, when the cedar rots out (this will happen mainly at the bottom) you won't have to replace the posts.

TIPS FOR SUCCESS

For some general suggestions on using these plans, see page 113.

■ **MATERIALS**

Three 8′ pressure-treated 4 × 4s.
Twenty-one 6″ #3-grade cedar 1 × 6s (see note page 5)
One lb. galvanized 6d box nails.

■ **DIRECTIONS**

Lay out the bins

1. Mark the center of the post holes in two rows of three, as shown in detail A.
2. Dig six post holes 12″ deep.

Build and install the back

3. Saw six 48″ posts from 4 × 4s.
4. Rip a 1 × 6 to make two pieces 2½″ wide. One is for the back siding; the other is for step 9.
5. Nail up the back with this ripping at the bottom and five 6′ 1 × 6s above it. The boards extend ⅞″ beyond both end posts. To check that the back is square, measure diagonally from corner to corner (in a rectangle, the diagonals are of equal length). Tack on a diagonal brace to hold everything square.
6. Slip the back assembly into the back holes. Brace the back end posts in the vertical position by pounding wooden stakes into the ground nearby and tacking angled pieces of wood between the stakes and the back assembly. Don't be tempted to skip the braces — they're essential.
7. When the back is braced plumb and horizontal, partly fill the three back holes with soil.

Compost Bins

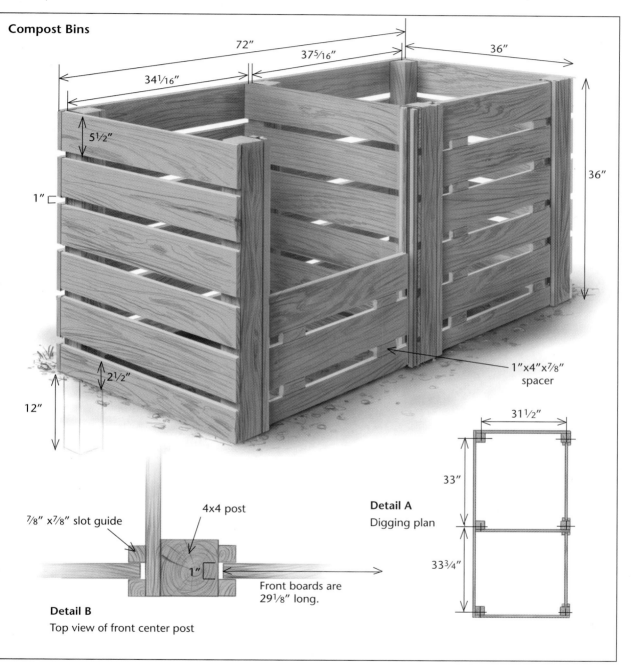

72"

37⁵⁄₁₆"

36"

34¹⁄₁₆"

5¹⁄₂"

1"

36"

2¹⁄₂"

12"

1"x4"x⁷⁄₈"
spacer

⁷⁄₈" x⁷⁄₈" slot guide

4x4 post

1"

Detail B
Top view of front center post

Front boards are
29¹⁄₈" long.

31¹⁄₂"

33"

Detail A
Digging plan

33³⁄₄"

Build the sides and center divider

8. Saw 16 pieces of 1×6 to $35\frac{1}{8}''$.

9. Rip one of these boards to $2\frac{1}{2}''$. From the remainder from step 4, cut two pieces $2\frac{1}{2}'' \times 35\frac{1}{8}''$. These three $2\frac{1}{2}''$ boards make the bottom course of siding for the ends and the center divider.

10. Tack two pieces from step 8 to one of the remaining posts, with the ends flush to the edge of the post. Place this post in a front corner hole and tack the other ends of the siding to the back post so that the overall front-to-back measurement is 36". Hint: A big C-clamp is quite handy for holding the siding to the post as you nail. Second-best hint: Lightly hold a second hammer behind the post to absorb the shock.

11. Using a carpenter's square, position the front corner post to make a square back corner.

12. Tack a diagonal brace between the front corner post and the center rear post.

13. Holding the front post so that it sticks out of the ground 36", brace it in vertical position.

14. Repeat steps 10 to 13 for the two remaining posts. Brace the center post diagonally to a back corner post.

15. Partly backfill the front holes and nail siding to the ends and center divider. Now remove the tacked-on siding.

Make the front

16. Rip eight pieces $\frac{7}{8}'' \times \frac{7}{8}'' \times 36''$ for the front slot guides.

17. Nail these rippings to the front posts (on one side of the center post, you'll be nailing through the siding into the post. The front ripping should be flush to the front of the post. Place the rear ripping so that you create a 1" vertical channel between the rippings.

18. Saw 11 pieces of 1×6 to $29\frac{1}{8}''$, then rip one twice to make two pieces $2\frac{1}{2}''$ wide. These are the removable front boards.

19. From scrap, prepare 20 spacers $1'' \times \frac{7}{8}'' \times 4''$. Screw these 2" from the end, on the bottom, of all $5\frac{1}{2}''$-wide front pieces. The 1" gap allows air to enter the compost, creating a healthy, aerobic environment.

20. Drop the removable fronts into position. If they are too tight, trim them.

21. Fill all holes with dirt and tamp with a length of 2×4 so the posts are tight.

Now that the bin is finished, follow the golden rules of composting. Avoid meat, and use the right proportion of "green" and "brown" materials. I also suggest using these rotten, homegrown tricks:

- When you add a lot of fresh stuff, spread around a shovelful of almost-finished compost on top to inoculate it with decay organisms.
- Occasionally stir the top 6″ of the first pile to get the decay started.
- Make a coarse-screened riddle (see page 32) so that when you remove finished compost, you can throw back stuff that hasn't rotted enough.

RIDDLE

My mother says you're supposed to use compost before it's fully rotted, but she doesn't say what to do about the clumps of partly digested yuck that abound in this compost. I finally concocted a funky-but-effective 23″-square riddle for quickly screening compost into the wheelbarrow. It's a hand-protective design, with the rough edges on the inside, where they can't cut you. Whatever doesn't fit through the riddle I immediately return for another run through the biological gauntlet called a compost pile.

I used 2″ × 2″ wire fencing for the mesh, but you could use finer mesh as well if you want to use the riddle for screening potting soil. You'll want a variable-speed drill with screwdriver bit and countersink.

■ MATERIALS

One 8′ #3-grade cedar 1 × 4
One 27″ × 27″ piece of wire mesh
Eight $2^1/_2$″ galvanized deck screws
Twenty-four $1^5/_8$″ deck screws ($1^1/_4$″ for $3/_4$″cedar lumber)
A handful of $3/_4$″ poultry staples

■ DIRECTIONS

1. Rip the 1 × 4 to $2^5/_8$″, leaving a remainder that's $3/_4$″ wide.
2. Saw four pieces $7/_8$″ × $2^5/_8$″ × 22″ for the frame.
3. Saw four pieces $7/_8$″ × $3/_4$″ × $19^3/_4$″ for the mesh retainers.

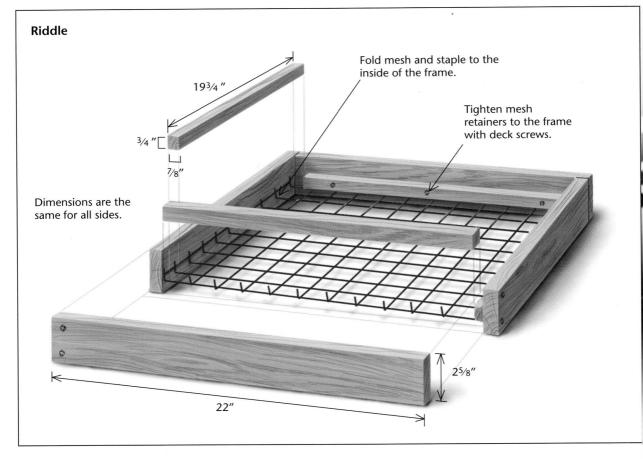

Riddle

19³⁄₄ "

³⁄₄ "

⁷⁄₈"

Dimensions are the same for all sides.

Fold mesh and staple to the inside of the frame.

Tighten mesh retainers to the frame with deck screws.

2⁵⁄₈"

22"

4. Assemble the frame from the 2⁵⁄₈" rippings, using two 2¹⁄₂" screws per end. The frame should be 22⁷⁄₈" square.

5. Cut the wire mesh to 25" square. Fold up the edges so that the mesh just fits inside the frame and the raw edges will be covered by the mesh retainers (step 7). Trim the mesh as needed.

6. Holding the staples with pliers to protect your fingers, staple the mesh inside the frame. Support the frame from behind so that you can drive the staples tight.

7. Place the mesh retainers over the mesh on the inside of the frame. Screw from inside with the 1⁵⁄₈" screws, making sure to cover all edges of the mesh.

COLD FRAME

Eager to extend your spring and fall growing seasons? That's a big concern where I live (on Wisconsin's virtual tundra). If you have the same problem, check out this novel, slopes-toward-the-sun design that reaches up toward whatever sunlight manages to reach your home place. I checked the unconventional sash angle with the Horticulture Department at the University of Wisconsin–Madison and found that they'd just built cold frames using the identical angle. They also told me that the high top creates an air space that allows overheated air to move away from the plants.

If you live in a state blessed with excess sunlight, you might want to reduce the sash angle by altering the shape of the plywood sides in step 1. Move the top corner of the sides down the dotted line shown in the plywood cutting diagram, and don't cut the front or back plywood pieces until it's time to fasten them. They will be smaller than shown in the plans, but the rest of the instructions still apply.

You'll need a circular saw with plywood and all-purpose blades. Since you'll screw this frame together (it's much stronger), you will appreciate having a variable-speed drill. Use appropriate protection when handling and sawing treated lumber — it's toxic.

■ MATERIALS

One sheet pressure-treated $1/2''$ plywood

Two 8′ pressure-treated 2 × 4s

One 8′ pressure-treated 1 × 8

One 4′ pressure-treated 1 × 4

Fiberglass greenhouse glazing to make two pieces 2′ × 4′, or one piece 4′ × 4′

One lb. $1\frac{5}{8}''$ rustproof deck screws

Twelve 2″ deck screws

Six 3″ deck screws

Twenty #6 × $3/4''$ galvanized round-head Phillips screws

Four $2\frac{1}{2}''$ galvanized butt hinges

Two $2\frac{1}{2}''$ galvanized tee hinges

Cold Frame

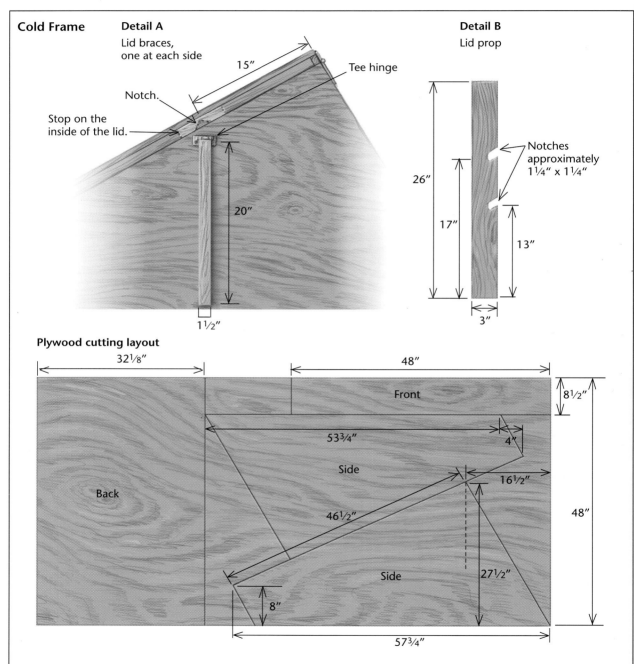

Detail A

Lid braces,
one at each side

15"

Notch.

Tee hinge

Stop on the
inside of the lid.

20"

1½"

Detail B

Lid prop

26"

17"

13"

Notches
approximately
1¼" x 1¼"

3"

Plywood cutting layout

32⅛"

48"

Front

8½"

53¾"

4"

Side

16½"

Back

46½"

48"

27½"

8"

Side

57¾"

■ DIRECTIONS

Build the body

1. Saw the plywood according to the pattern, making two sides, the front, and the back.

2. From 2 × 4, saw the back crossbar (44″ long) and two side rails. Make the side rails as long as the plywood sides, and take their end angles from the plywood sides. The end angles of the side rails are different, and neither is square.

3. Fasten the side rails to the back crossbar with two 3″ screws per joint, making a frame 47″ wide.

4. Attach the sides to this frame with a $1^5/8$″ screw every 8″. Then screw the back flush to the sides and the back crossbar.

5. Rip a 40″ 2 × 4 down the $3^1/2$″ face to make two pieces $1^1/2$″ × $1^5/8$″. The rippings make the two back and two front braces. Hold them in place, mark, and cut to length.

6. Screw the back and sides to the back braces, which will butt up to the side rail. Screw the front edge of the sides flush to the front braces, which butt up to the side rail.

7. Screw the front plywood to the front braces.

8. Saw the front crossbar, $3/4$″ × $1^1/2$″ × 44″. Hold the crossbar between the side rails, flush to the top of the side rails, with the $1^1/2$″ face up. Screw through the front plywood into the crossbar. Hint: Clamp the pieces to simplify this step.

Build the lid

9. From $3/4$″ × $1^1/2$″ material, saw two 48″ and three $46^1/2$″ pieces. Assemble the lid so that it's 48″ square, with the shorter rippings placed between the two longer ones, and the $3/4$″ faces up. Use two 2″ screws per joint.

10. Cut the fiberglass greenhouse glazing to size and rest it on the lid. The joint between sheets (if there is one) should overlap in the center bar. Sandpaper the edges smooth.

11. Saw three 48″ lid battens from $3/4$″ × $3/4$″ material. Predrill (preferably with a countersink) and screw the battens to the lid about every 6″ with $1^5/8$″ deck screws. Use a few $3/4$″ #6 galvanized round-head Phillips screws to hold the glazing to the top and bottom lid bars.

Cold Frame

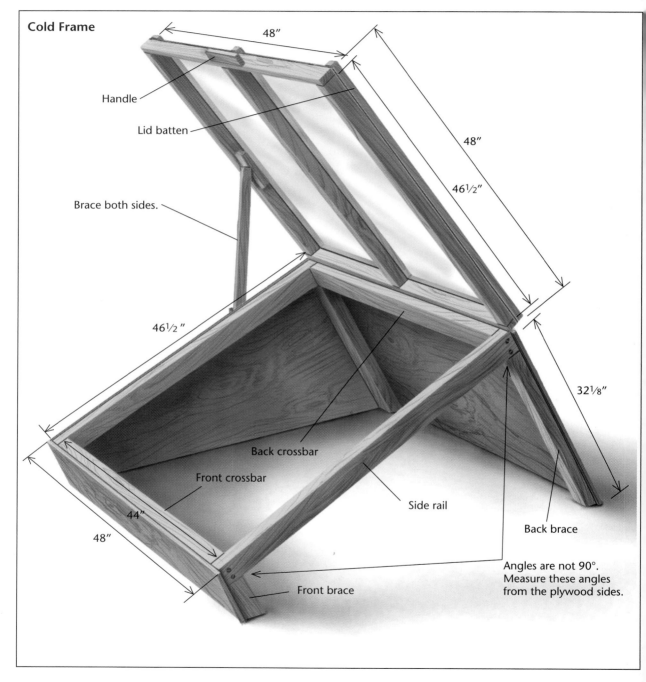

Handle

Lid batten

Brace both sides.

48"

48"

46½"

46½"

32⅛"

Back crossbar

Front crossbar

Side rail

Back brace

44"

48"

Front brace

Angles are not 90°.
Measure these angles
from the plywood sides.

12. Distribute four butt hinges across the back of the lid to hold it to the back, and screw. Use a few $1^5/8''$ screws on the lower half of the hinges to fasten into the back crossbar.

Finish up

13. Saw a handle, $3'' \times {}^3/_4'' \times 8''$, and screw it to the center bottom of the lid, with the $^3/_4''$ side against the lid.

14. Saw two braces, $1^1/2'' \times 20''$, and screw them to narrow end of the tee hinges. See detail A. Screw one hinge to each side, 15″ down from the upper corner so that the braces can swing into the vertical position.

15. Saw a $^1/_4''$ deep × 1″ wide notch into the lid side rails, directly above each brace from step 14. The braces will rest here to support the lid when raised.

16. Saw two $2'' \times {}^3/_4'' \times 6''$ stops. Screw them inside the lid frame, next to the notch, to prevent the braces from slipping.

17. Saw the lid prop shown in detail B on page 35. To hold the lid open so that your plants won't cook on sunny days, simply slip the handle into a notch on the prop.

18. Install the frame:

    a) Dig out a bed about 6″ deep, and set the frame into it. This will insulate the frame, but your plants will be harder to reach; or

    b) Set the frame directly on the ground. The plants will be more accessible, but weeds may creep in around the edges and the plants will not stay as warm; or

    c) Make a rectangular ground frame from 2 × 2s, $54^3/4'' \times 48''$ on the outside. (This wood is not in the materials list; use scrap if you have it.) Place this frame on the ground, and the cold frame atop it. When the ground frame rots, just replace it.

TRANSPLANT SHELTER

Here's a simple-minded but handy item for protecting vulnerable transplants from harsh sun and hard rain. This shelter folds for storage and should last a dozen years, particularly if you can find it an inside home during the off-season. I made the crossbars from scrap wood lath, saving money and a tiny bit of the planet at the same time, but you can also make them from 1 × 2s.

Transplant Shelter

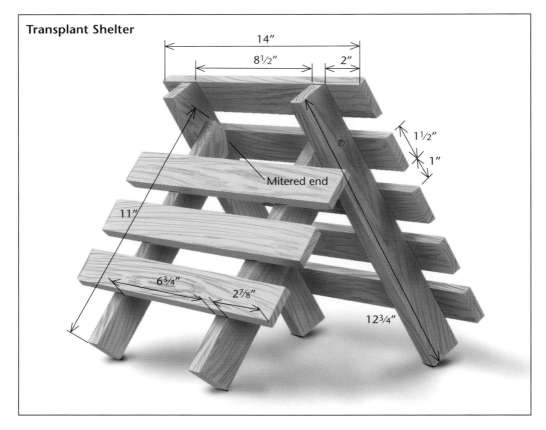

14″

8½″

2″

1½″

1″

Mitered end

11″

6¾″

2⅞″

12¾″

- **MATERIALS**

Crossbars: three 4′ laths ($\frac{3}{8}$″ × $1\frac{1}{2}$″), or one 10′ 1 × 2

Uprights: one 4′ 1 × 3

Two $1\frac{5}{8}$″ rustproof screws

A handful of galvanized nails (3d for lath crossbars, 4d for 1 × 2 crossbars)

- **DIRECTIONS**

1. Cut eight 14″ crossbars from laths or 1 × 2.

2. Cut two uprights 13″ long, and two 11″ long.

3. Cut off (miter) one corner of each shorter upright.

4. Assemble the short side so that the uprights are $2\frac{7}{8}$″ from the end of the lath, using two nails per joint.

5. Repeat for the longer side, with 2″ clearance at the ends.

6. Nest the sides together. Drill a ⅛″ hole near the top of each longer upright. Drive a screw through the hole, into the shorter upright, for a hinge.

PLANT SUPPORTS

Pity the pathetic cucumber, clematis, and tomato — they just don't have the backbone to hold themselves above the ground. Your options: curse their spinelessness, or build them a wooden vertebral column. That's easier than it sounds, and it will liberate you from those wretched wire thingamabobs some false prophet claimed would guide your plants up toward the sun.

Wood Trellis

Here's a trellis that's ideal for helping morning glories or clematis climb a chimney or festoon a fading fence. Build several, and you might even start to forget that home-sweet-home is slathered with homely aluminum siding. I designed the trellis 8′ tall by 56″ wide at the top, but you can adapt it to virtually any size. You'll need a circular saw or a table saw, and a countersink for your drill.

- **MATERIALS**

One 8′ #3-grade cedar 1 × 10 (see note page 113). Make sure the cedar is not too knotty.

One 10″ piece of 1 × 6 cedar

One sheet medium sandpaper

Fifty 1¼″ rustproof deck screws

Four sets of mounting hardware (screws for shingles, wood, aluminum, or vinyl siding; lag screws and shields for masonry).

- **DIRECTIONS**

1. Rip eight ⅝″ strips for the side uprights and angle braces, and one 1½″ strip for the center upright (all uprights are 8′ long). Sandpaper all pieces.

2. Position the center upright at the center of the base plate and at a right angle to it, with the bottoms flush. Countersink and fasten with two screws.

3. Position six $5/8'' \times 7/8''$ uprights on the base plate so that the $5/8''$ side faces you, and spread the tops as shown. Then fasten each upright to the base plate with one screw placed 1″ from the bottom and slightly staggered.

4. Mark 4″ down from the top of the right upright, and $36 1/2''$ down from the top of the left upright.

5. Place one $5/8'' \times 7/8''$ strip diagonally across the trellis to these marks, with the $5/8''$ side facing you. This is the top brace.

6. Mark and cut the ends of the top brace, and return it to position. After checking that all uprights are 9″ on center (measured across the top), countersink and screw the top brace to each upright.

7. Mark $7 1/2''$ below where the top brace crosses the center upright. Place a $5/8'' \times 7/8''$ strip on this mark, parallel to the top brace. Cut to length and screw into position.

8. Repeat step 7 for the last two braces.

9. Drive a second screw to fasten each upright to the base plate. Stagger these screws to prevent splitting.

10. Cut the sides of the base plate flush with the outside uprights.

11. Make spacers to hold the trellis away from the wall by ripping a piece $7/8'' \times 1 1/2''$ to 16″ long.

12. Saw two 3″ lengths from this ripping, and screw them to the back of the center upright, behind the bottom and top braces.

13. Hold the remainder of this ripping along the top rear of the base plate. Mark the ends, cut to size, and screw to the back of the base plate.

14. Mount with two screws through the base-plate spacer and one through each of the upper spacers. Be sure to screw into the studs on a frame house.

Beanpoles

Almost anything will do when it comes to beanpoles — an arbor fastened to the garage, a wire fence, strings tied vertically to whatever's handy, even the tomato trellises we'll build shortly. I advocate a tripod of bamboo poles, tied at the top with an exceedingly handy knot called the constrictor. This bulldog, a favorite of Clifford Ashley, American knotmaster extraordinaire, is also good for closing bags — and for homemade handcuffs.

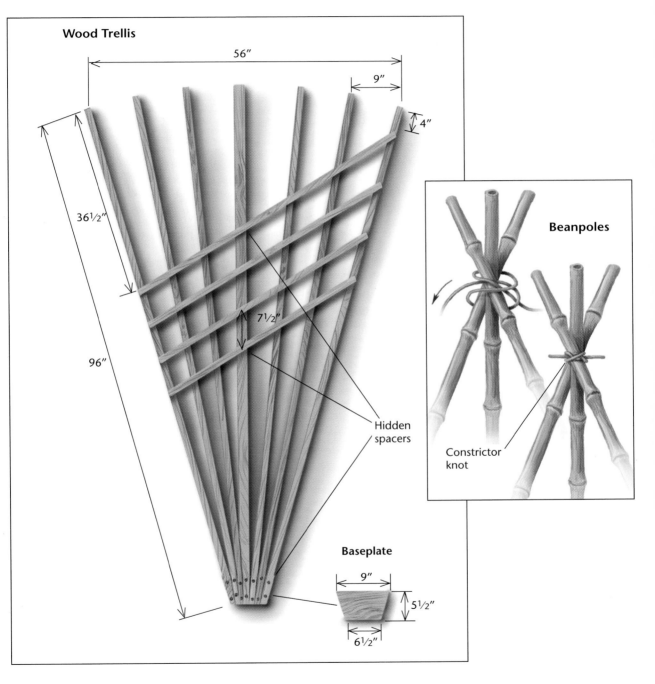

Wood Trellis

56"

9"

4"

36½"

7½"

96"

Hidden
spacers

Beanpoles

Constrictor
knot

Baseplate

9"

5½"

6½"

Tomato Trellis

It's summer, and it's business-as-usual in my son Alexander's garden. The tomatoes are vining, and I'm busy doing something — anything — except erecting my stone-age tomato trellises. Not that they helped much: circular trellises flipped over. Fence posts and hog wire worked great but were a nuisance to set up and, at best, as ugly as a hog.

So I concocted this preposterously simple tomato trellis, then found it equally effective for squashes, cucumbers, melons, and pole beans. Quickly made from cheap or recycled wood, this A-frame design is easy to use and simple to store. The model shown is 24″ wide and stands about 26″ high in the garden, but on this project, the dimensions are not sacred; if you need something larger or smaller, rejigger the dimensions to suit. To use, simply place over a tomato plant and pull vines through as they grow.

■ MATERIALS

One 10′ 1 × 3 (for the uprights)
Five 4′ laths ($3/8″ × 11/2″$), or one 8′ and one 10′ 1 × 2 (for the crossbars and brace)
Two $11/2″$ rustproof screws
A handful of galvanized nails (3d for lath crossbar, 6d for 1 × 2 crossbar).

■ DIRECTIONS

1. Saw two tall uprights, $313/4″$ long, from 1 × 3.
2. Saw two short uprights, $273/4″$ long, from 1 × 3.
3. Saw seven crossbars, $233/4″$ long, from lath or 1 × 2.
4. Nail the crossbars to the uprights with two nails per joint.
5. Fasten the brace to the long side, nailing only into the uprights. Trim the ends of the brace flush to the uprights. (If you're expecting a bin-buster crop, put another brace on the short side.)
6. When both sides are assembled, nest them inside each other. With the trellis folded up, drill a $1/8″$ hole 1″ from the top of the short uprights. Drive a screw through this hole, into the long upright, for a hinge.

Tomato Trellis

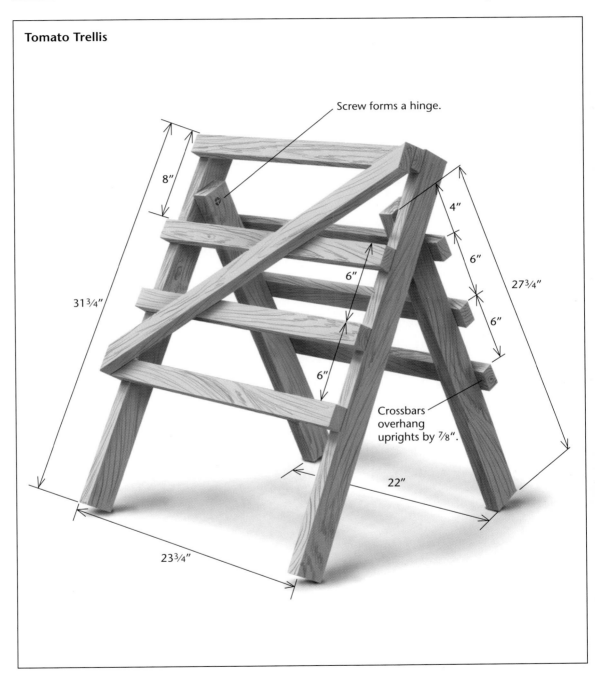

Screw forms a hinge.

8"

4"

6"

6"

27¾"

6"

6"

31¾"

6"

Crossbars
overhang
uprights by ⅞".

22"

23¾"

CHAPTER 3:

FOR THE ANIMALS

As countless books now remind us, gardens are not just for plants, but also for animals. Some people think sheltering birds, bats, and butterflies is a matter of ecological sanity — a tiny, but nevertheless useful, vote for biodiversity. Others welcome these flying friends for their aesthetic value as ephemeral flashes of color that can match the beauty of the finest rose or Japanese lantern. No matter which camp you're in, it helps to make a welcoming gesture. Nothing fancy, mind you — these flying garden ornaments seem to know that it's the intention, not the price tag, that counts.

PAINTED BIRDHOUSE

Sometimes, the only thing a garden needs is a stylish birdhouse. If that's your problem, you've come to the right page. You will need a $1\frac{1}{4}''$ hole saw. One note of caution: if you don't predrill the nail holes, you'll end up splitting that luscious red cedar. Curses!

■ **MATERIALS**

One 6′ #3-grade cedar 1 × 8 (see note page 5)
A few 6d galvanized nails
Two $1\frac{5}{8}''$ deck screws
One $2\frac{1}{2}''$ deck screw
Exterior paint as desired

Painted birdhouse: Even if the paint doesn't fool the birds, it does dress up the birdhouse.

■ **DIRECTIONS**

1. Rip a 26″ board to 6³⁄₄″ for the front and back.
2. Mark the middle of each end and miter down 45° in both directions.
3. Crosscut this board to make identical pieces 12¹⁄₄″ tall.
4. On the center of the front, drill a 1¹⁄₄″ entry hole, centered at 6³⁄₄″ above the bottom.

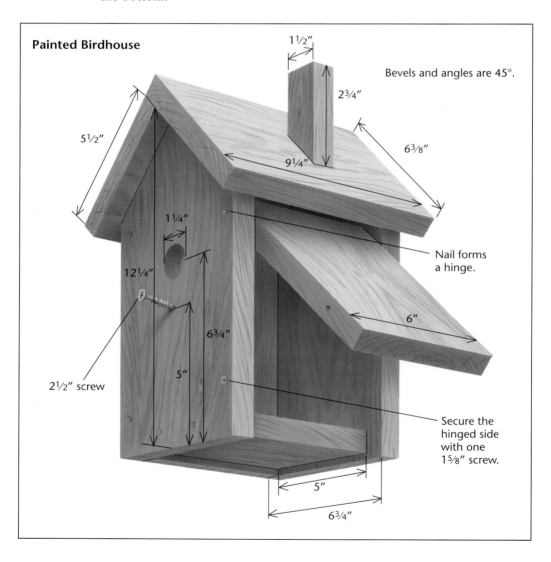

Painted Birdhouse

Bevels and angles are 45°.

Nail forms a hinge.

Secure the hinged side with one 1⁵⁄₈″ screw.

2¹⁄₂″ screw

5. Bevel the tops of two 10″ × 6″ boards at 45°. These make the sides.

6. Hold each side in position against the front. With the tops flush, mark the bottom of each side, and saw it.

7. Nail through the front and back to the sides. To make one side pivot so that you can clean house, use a screw at the bottom front instead of a nail.

8. Saw the bottom 5″ × 6″. Nail it into position, $^1/_4$″ up from the bottom of the box. Do not nail into the pivoting side. Drill two $^1/_8$″ drain holes in bottom.

9. Saw the roofs $5^1/_2$″ × $9^1/_4$″ and $6^3/_8$″ × $9^1/_4$″.

10. Saw the chimney $^3/_4$″ × $1^1/_2$″ × $2^3/_4$″ high. Miter the bottom at 45°, and nail it to the wider roof board.

11. Nail down the roof boards with equal front and back overhangs.

12. Drive the $2^1/_2$″ deck screw into place for the perch.

13. Prime and paint to suit your fancy.

> **TIPS FOR SUCCESS**
>
> For some general suggestions on using these plans, see page 113.

WREN HOUSE

Who can resist the song of a house wren, a bird that's equally at home in woodland clearings and backyards? Not I (or my cat, Pupcat, who's now wearing three bells on his collar to scare off these tasty songsters). You could easily make this pleasant little home with a hand saw, but you will definitely need a 1″ hole saw or drill bit for the opening.

■ **MATERIALS**

One 5′ #3-grade cedar 1 × 8 (see note page 5)
A handful of 6d galvanized siding or box nails
One $1^1/_2$″ rustproof screw (for the door hinge)
Two $2^1/_2$″ screws (for mounting)

■ **DIRECTIONS**

1. Rip a 25″ board to 4″ for the back, front, and bottom.

2. Set your saw at 25° and bevel the top of the back so that it's $12^1/_4$″ at the longest dimension.

Wren House

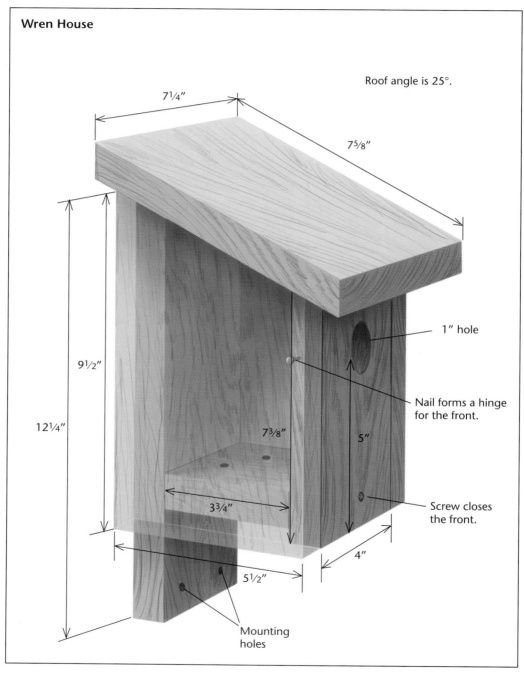

Roof angle is 25°.

7¼"

7⅝"

1" hole

Nail forms a hinge for the front.

9½"

12¼"

7⅜"

5"

Screw closes the front.

3¾"

4"

5½"

Mounting holes

3. Bevel the top of the front to $7^3/8''$ at the longest dimension.

4. Bevel both ends of the roof to make it $7^5/8''$ long by $7^1/4''$ wide.

5. Start the sides by ripping a 19″ board to $5^1/2''$. Miter across the middle at 25°, then crosscut the bottoms to make the sides $9^1/2''$ tall at the longest point.

6. Nail the sides to the back, with the top corners and rear edges flush.

7. Saw the bottom $3^3/4'' \times 4''$ and nail into position, $3/8''$ up from the bottom of the sides.

8. Mark the 1″ entry hole centered and 5″ from the bottom of the front. Place a scrap of wood under the front (to give a clean hole), and drill the hole.

9. Nail the sides to the front, using one nail per side placed about 5″ from the bottom. The nails make hinges so that the front will open at housecleaning time.

10. Countersink the $1^1/2''$ screw through the front into the bottom. This screw closes the front.

11. Cut the roof. Nail into position with equal side overhangs, flush to the back.

12. Drill two $3/16''$ holes for drainage in the bottom. Drill two $1/8''$ holes in the lower back for mounting.

13. Mount the house 5′ to 6′ above the ground with the $2^1/2''$ screws, preferably where cats can't sneak up on your tenants.

House for Chickadees, Titmice, and Nuthatches

Forget vinyl siding — these woodland birds prefer a natural approach to housing, in the form of a cedar, pine, basswood, or birch log. If you use cedar lumber instead of plywood for the top and bottom, predrill nail holes to prevent splitting the wood.

■ MATERIALS

One log, 6″ diameter by 15″ long

One 16″ cedar #3-grade 1 × 8 (or substitute $1/2''$ exterior plywood)

Four 2″ rustproof screws

Ten 8d galvanized siding nails

Two $1/4'' \times 3''$ lag bolts with flat washers (for mounting)

House for Chickadees, Titmice, and Nuthatches

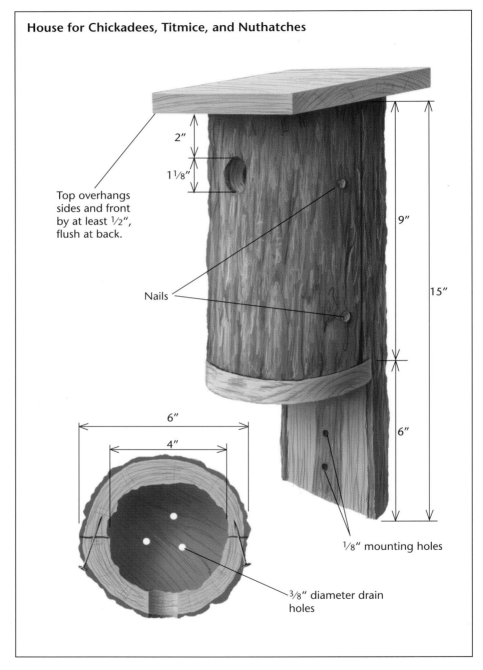

Top overhangs sides and front by at least ½", flush at back.

2"

1⅛"

9"

15"

6"

Nails

6"

4"

⅛" mounting holes

⅜" diameter drain holes

■ **DIRECTIONS**

1. Cut the log so that the top will slope slightly to the front for drainage.

2. Crosscut the log at 9″ from the top, but stop 1″ to 1¹⁄₂″ before cutting all the way through.

3. Split the upper part of the log in half, using an ax, saw, or wedges.

4. Flatten the bottom section by making parallel saw cuts and then chiseling away the waste.

5. Hollow out the upper section with a hammer and chisel, making a master bedroom about 4″ in diameter. If you have a gouge (a rounded chisel), it's ideal for this job.

6. Drill a 1¹⁄₈″ entry hole 2″ from the top.

7. Predrill holes and nail the log back together.

8. Hold the bottom against the lower end of the log, and mark the log shape on it. Cut with a saber or coping saw. (This step is purely decorative — a square bottom will function just as well if you're feeling lazy or don't have the right saw.)

9. Drill three ³⁄₈″ drainage holes in the bottom, and nail it snugly in the position.

10. Saw the top so that it overhangs the log by at least ¹⁄₂″ at the front and sides.

11. Add a bit of coarse sawdust for bedding, and fasten the top with four screws.

12. Drill mounting holes through the bottom stub, and mount with the lag bolts in a sheltered location, with the opening away from prevailing winter winds. Mount the house 3′ to 10′ above the ground for chickadees; 6′ to 10′ for titmice; and 10′ to 20′ for nuthatches.

ROBIN HOUSE

Robins prefer open-air housing, the kind of exposure to nature I appreciate only on a tropical beach. If you mount this highly ventilated dwelling under the eaves, or in a protected part of a tree, you might be lucky enough to attract barn swallows. Even though the robins probably won't appreciate it, I added eaves, overhangs, and reliefs to alleviate boxiness. Overall, the house is 15″ tall by 11″ wide by 10″ deep. You'll appreciate a circular saw and a drill for making pilot holes for nails to prevent splitting.

■ MATERIALS

One 6′ #3-grade cedar 1 × 12 (see note page 5)
A handful of 3d galvanized lath nails
A handful of 6d or 8d galvanized siding nails
Two 2¹⁄₂″ deck screws for mounting.

■ DIRECTIONS

1. Start the back by sawing a 1 × 12 to 14¹⁄₂″ long. Rip it to 8⁷⁄₈″ wide.
2. Mark the top center of the back, and miter downward 45° in each direction.
3. Crosscut the bottom of the back so that it's 14″ tall at the peak.
4. Rip a 24″ board to 8″ for the sides. With the saw set at 45°, miter across the center to make two pieces, each about 12″ long and beveled at the top.
5. With the saw set at 90°, cut the bottom of the sides so that they are 10⁵⁄₈″ long at the longest dimension.
6. Nail through the back into the sides with two nails per joint. Note that the sides are inset ¹⁄₄″ from the back.
7. Saw the floor 6⁵⁄₈″ × 10¹⁄₈″.
8. Saw the front edging, 6⁵⁄₈″ × 2¹⁄₄″, and nail it flush to the front of the floor with 3d nails.
9. Nail through the sides and back into the floor so that the sides extend ³⁄₈″ below the floor.
10. Rip a 16″ 1 × 12 to 10″ wide for the roofs. Crosscut at a 45° bevel across the middle. Then crosscut again to make one piece 6³⁄₄″ long, and the other 7⁵⁄₈″ long, measuring on the shorter faces.
11. Nail the roof pieces together at the top, and rest the roof on the house, flush with the back. Check that it resembles the picture (mine didn't on the first try). If everything is kosher, nail the roof down.
12. Drill four ³⁄₁₆″ holes in the bottom for drainage.
13. Drill two ¹⁄₈″ holes in the back, and fasten the box to a tree or under friendly overhang, at least 10′ to 12′ above the ground.

Robin House

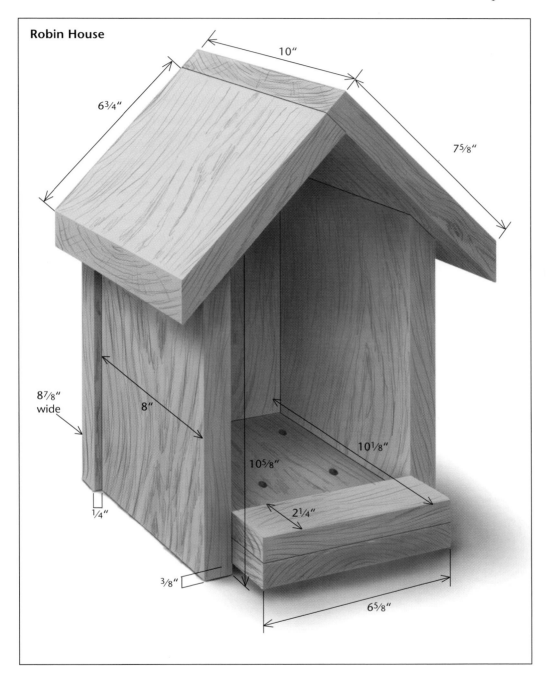

10"

6³⁄₄"

7⁵⁄₈"

8⁷⁄₈"
wide

8"

10¹⁄₈"

10⁵⁄₈"

2¹⁄₄"

¹⁄₄"

³⁄₈"

6⁵⁄₈"

GOURD HOUSE FOR PURPLE MARTIN

Purple martins are the classic organic bug-bane, the friend of all who call the mosquito enemy. The good news is that if you plan ahead, you can keep the cedar trees where they belong — in the forests — and still give purple martins a backyard home. The bad news, of course, is that you'll have to plant birdhouse gourd seeds a growing season ahead. Let the gourds dry until the seeds shake, then cut a 2″ entry hole about 4″ from the bottom. Use a paring knife to shape the hole so that it's slightly oval, which the martins apparently find more convenient. Don't bother placing a perch below the hole — martins don't need it.

With a ¼″ bit, drill a few ventilation and drainage holes around the top and bottom. Drill another hole at the top to hold a wire for stringing up the gourd. Now hang the gourd about 20′ above the ground (see the martin house pole project, following, for further suggestions on locating the houses).

MARTIN HOUSE POLE

Martins like to live well above predators, meaning their houses need a tall pole. And since you're supposed to take their houses down in the fall for cleaning, you want an apparatus that allows convenient raising and lowering.

Because martins prefer a clear flight path, try to locate the house more than 40′ from obstructions. If this is impossible, make the pole toward the tall end of the 12′ to 18′ range listed below. Martins like to live in groups, so you can hang the gourds condo-style, 1′ apart on the crossbar. If you're using this pole for a conventional martin house, just omit the crossbar and brace.

By the way, it's best to not erect the houses until a month after martins arrive. Otherwise, English sparrows and other unwanted guests might monopolize your gourdian birdhouses.

You'll need a ½″ drill bit that can cut 12″ deep and a crosscut saw capable of cutting 3½″ lumber. To saw threaded rod, thread a nut next to the cut location, then clamp the nut in a vise and saw next to it with a fine-toothed hacksaw.

■ MATERIALS

(all wood is CCA-treated to prevent decay)
One 4 × 4 of each: 8′, 10′, and 12′ to 18′
One 6′ 2 × 4

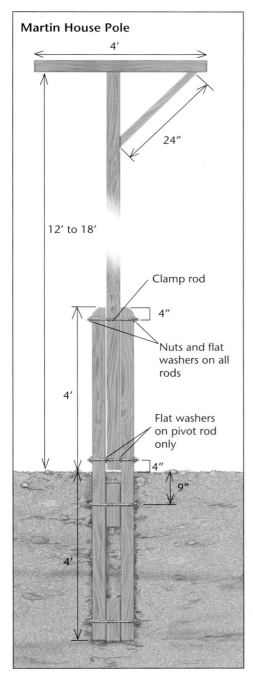

Martin House Pole

4'

24"

12' to 18'

Clamp rod

4"

Nuts and flat
washers on all
rods

4'

Flat washers
on pivot rod
only

4"

9"

4'

Gourd birdhouse: _If you don't feel like building an
elaborate pole for purple martins, try using an obliging tree._

Four 12″ pieces of ¹/₂″-diameter threaded rod, with 8 nuts and 10 flat washers, all galvanized

Nine 2¹/₂″ rustproof deck screws

■ **DIRECTIONS**

1. From the 10′ 4 × 4, saw two 12″ spacer blocks.
2. Using the remainder from step 1, and the 8′ 4 × 4, make two support posts. Shape the tops as shown.
3. Drill a ¹/₂″ hole through the support posts and spacers at the locations shown. Loosely bolt the spacers between the posts, using a flat washer under these and all other nuts.
4. Screw a 48″ 2 × 4 crossbar flat on top of the pole.
5. Saw 45° bevels on both ends of a 24″ 2 × 4 for the diagonal brace.
6. Fasten the brace to the pole and crossbar with three screws per joint.
7. Put the bottom of the pole between the support posts. Drill the pivot hole 52″ from the bottom of the support posts and 3″ from the bottom of the pole.
8. Feed a 12″ threaded rod through this hole. Place a flat washer between the pole and each post, and loosely tighten. These washers serve as bearings so that the pole can swing freely on this pivot rod.
9. Align the pole and supports straight (with the structure on the ground), and drill the upper hole. Insert the clamp rod, which holds the pole in upright position, and install washers and nuts.
10. Tighten all nuts, particularly on the two below-ground rods.
11. Optional: paint or stain the pole, crossbar, and above-ground sections of the support posts.
12. Dig a hole 4′ deep and large enough for the support posts. Make sure you select a location where the pole can be lowered without obstructions.
13. With the pole lowered, brace the support posts in vertical position, and tamp the backfill with a hunk of 2 × 4. For the best stability, backfill with concrete and let set for one week.
14. Hang the gourds 1′ apart on the crossbar and raise the pole.

Save that tree stump for something useful — like mounting a birdhouse.

WINDOW FEEDER

If you're lucky enough to have old-fashioned double-hung windows that actually work, you can set up a birdie delicatessen right outside your window — close enough to watch but easy to fill and relatively safe from hungry cats. (Unfortunately, you can't pull off this trick with casement windows, since they swing out.) You'll need a table saw, circular saw, or router to cut the channels for the bin fronts, and a countersink. You can cut the acrylic sheeting with a table saw, or ask a hardware store to do it. Predrill the nail holes to prevent splitting.

■ MATERIALS

One 8′ #3-grade cedar 1 × 8 (see note page 5)
One $4^1/_4″ \times 15″ \times ^1/_4″$ exterior plywood (for the bin backs)
One $5″ \times 16″ \times ^1/_8″$ clear acrylic sheet (for the bin fronts)
A handful each of $1^5/_8″$ rustproof screws, 6d galvanized siding nails, and tacks
Two $1^1/_2 \times 2″$ galvanized or brass hinges with screws
Two galvanized 4″ "L" brackets

■ DIRECTIONS

Start the bottom

1. Saw the bottom 6″ × 22″.
2. Cut two 18″ pieces of 1 × 8 and rip a $1^1/_2″$ piece from each one. Save the narrow rippings for the skirts (step 11).

Prepare the end assemblies

3. From the remainder from step 2, saw four sides with the tops and inner edges mitered at 15°. Study the drawing so that the good face will be out on each side.
4. If you have a table saw, set the depth to $^5/_{16}″$, and saw a channel for the bin fronts on the inside of each side. Otherwise, use a router or circular saw to cut channels about $^1/_8″$ wide.
5. Put a tack $^3/_4″$ up from the bottom of each slot so that the bin fronts stay up and the opening stays open.
6. Saw two ends $4^1/_4″$ wide × $6^3/_4″$ tall (measured at the shorter dimension), with the top beveled at 15°.

7. Nail up each end assembly with the bottoms of the pieces flush (the end assembly rests on the feeder's bottom).

8. Saw two bin backs from $1/4''$ plywood, $41/4'' \times 7''$.

9. Tack the bin backs into position so that the seed will slide toward the opening as it falls.

10. Position each end assembly on the bottom, and countersink and screw from below.

Finish up

11. Saw a 15° miter on one end of each piece remaining from step 2 to make the skirts. Put the skirts into position, mark the other ends to length, and miter them.

12. Screw the skirts into position from below.

13. Saw two lids, with both ends mitered, $61/2''$ long $\times 63/4''$ wide.

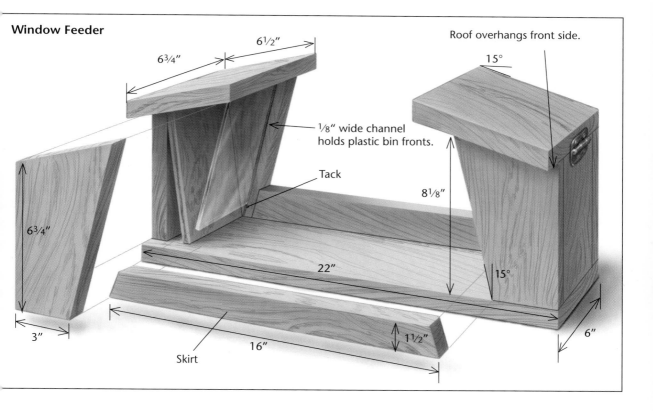

Window Feeder

Roof overhangs front side.

$61/2''$

$63/4''$

15°

$1/8''$ wide channel holds plastic bin fronts.

Tack

$81/8''$

$63/4''$

22"

15°

3"

16"

$11/2''$

6"

Skirt

14. Fasten the hinges to the lids. The lids should be flush to the house side and overhanging on the outside.

15. Cut or buy two pieces of acrylic sheet 7$\frac{1}{2}$″ long × 4$\frac{3}{4}$″ wide for the bin fronts (Note: Check that this will fit the actual width of your slots and adjust dimensions if necessary). Sandpaper the edges of the plastic smooth, and slip the fronts into place.

16. Mount the feeder on galvanized angle brackets fastened to your window sill.

SUET FEEDER FOR WOODPECKERS

For woodpeckers and other birds that are unchic enough to prefer a high-fat diet, you'll have to bring out the suet, and that means you've got to buy or make a suet feeder. This simple contraption, which gives woodpeckers a place to rest their tails while feasting, is so fast and inexpensive that you could easily make several and give some away.

■ **MATERIALS**

One 2′ #3-grade cedar 1 × 6 (for once, the thickness does not matter)
One 8″ × 16″ piece of 1″ × 1″ rust-resistant mesh
Six 2″ deck screws
Eight $\frac{3}{4}$″ galvanized staples
5′ of $\frac{1}{8}$″ rope suitable for outdoor use

■ **DIRECTIONS**

1. Saw the four pieces of the frame: two 2″ × 9″ (for the crossbars), and two 2″ × 7″ (for the uprights).

2. Optional: Saw two $\frac{1}{4}$″ dadoes as wide as your wood is thick in the bottom crossbar. Locate the outside edge of each dado $\frac{3}{4}$″ from the end of the crossbar.

3. Screw the tail rest to the bottom crossbar, centered and flush to the rear.

4. Screw both uprights into the dadoes made in step 2 (if you didn't bother with dadoes, just screw the uprights $\frac{3}{4}$″ from the end of the lower crossbar).

5. Drill four $\frac{3}{16}$″ holes in the upper crossbar and the uprights, and thread the

rope through them so that the feeder's weight will hold it closed. Knot the rope on the inside of the uprights.

6. Cut two pieces of mesh big enough to overlap each frame piece about $1/2''$. Place the frame on good support, and staple the mesh to the front, and then the back, of the frame. Don't staple the mesh to the top crossbar.

7. Hang the feeder on a handy branch in a sheltered location.

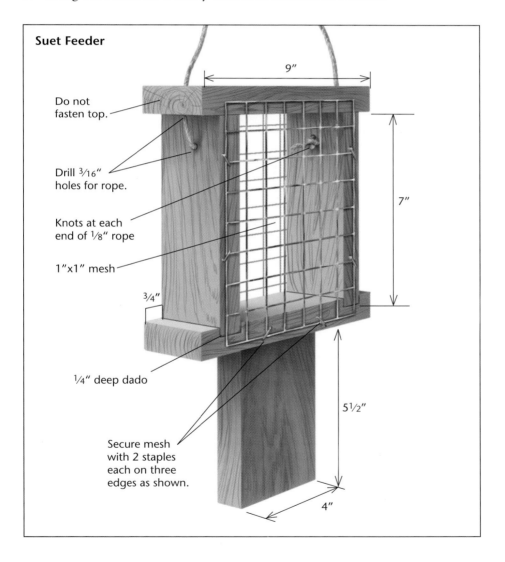

Suet Feeder

9"

Do not fasten top.

Drill $3/16''$ holes for rope.

Knots at each end of $1/8''$ rope

1"x1" mesh

7"

$3/4''$

$1/4''$ deep dado

Secure mesh with 2 staples each on three edges as shown.

$5\,1/2''$

4"

BIRDBATH

One of the best ways to attract birds is to offer them a private backyard spa. This concrete birdbath is formed inside a round, 26″-diameter plastic "saucer" that's sold as a sled. You'll need tin snips, a trowel with one curved edge, gloves, and a way to mix concrete (ideally, a wheelbarrow and hoe). If you want, you can wet the finished birdbath and paint it with exterior latex paint, either full-strength or diluted. Suggestions on mounting the bath follow the instructions; for a hanging bath, you'll need to cast eye bolts into the concrete.

■ MATERIALS

$1^3/_4″ \times 77″$ galvanized steel or aluminum sheet metal (preferably steel, which is much stiffer)
Three sheet metal screws
Enough $2″ \times 2″$ steel fencing to make three 21″-diameter disks
About 100 lbs. of bagged concrete mix

■ DIRECTIONS

Make the form

1. Cut a $1^3/_4″ \times 77″$ ribbon of sheet metal for the outer form, and bend it into a circle with the ends overlapping 5″. Fasten the overlap with three sheet metal screws, making a form 23″ in diameter.
2. Make a 21″-diameter paper template as a guide for cutting three disks of reinforcement from the fencing.
3. Cut the disks and press them into a concave shape that conforms to the saucer. Bend the edges of the disks so that they stay at least 1″ from the outer form. Work carefully, as it's impossible to push the reinforcement back into the wet concrete.
4. Grease the form and the saucer with motor oil so that the concrete won't stick.
5. Place the form inside the saucer, making it as circular as possible.

Pour the concrete

6. Mix bagged concrete with the minimum amount of water.
7. Add a bit of concrete to the bottom of the saucer, and position the first reinforcement disk. Continue adding mix and disks, making sure the disks neither touch the form and saucer nor poke through the top.

8. Tap the saucer and the outer form with a hammer so that concrete fills the voids. Don't let the concrete puddle to the center or your bath won't hold much water — keep an even thickness all around. Use the outer form as a guide for smoothing the concrete with a curved-edge trowel.

9. Continue smoothing the top by troweling (that's a kind of circular massage). Trowel again every few minutes to draw cement paste into the gaps between the stones in the concrete and make a smooth surface.

10. Place a small container of water next to the bath, and cover both with plastic so that the concrete will stay damp while curing. Allow the bath to set for a week before moving. If you want a stony exterior, gently remove the bath from the form after three days and wire brush the outside. Knock off the rough edges of concrete before use.

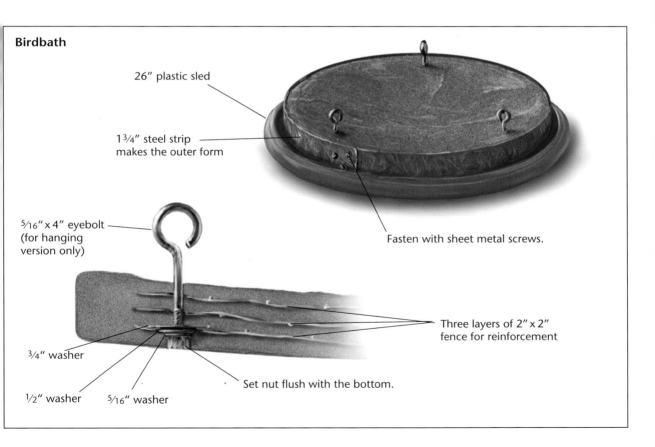

Birdbath

26" plastic sled

1¾" steel strip makes the outer form

⁵⁄₁₆" x 4" eyebolt (for hanging version only)

Fasten with sheet metal screws.

Three layers of 2" x 2" fence for reinforcement

¾" washer

½" washer   ⁵⁄₁₆" washer

Set nut flush with the bottom.

Mounting options:

- Place the bath on the ground (recommended only where cats are scarce);
- Rest the bath on a 2′ long by 10″ diameter round flue tile. Place the large end of the tile down and partly fill it with stones for stability; or
- Hang the bath from a tree, using three sets of this galvanized hardware: a $5/16″ \times 31/2″$ eye bolt with nut, and $3/4″$, $1/2″$, and $5/16″$ flat washers. You'll also need one $3/8″ \times 31/2″$ screw eye for mounting to the tree, five substantial S hooks, and, depending on the height of the branch, at least 15′ of $1/4″$ chain. Here's how:

Adapt the above technique to cast the eye bolts into the birdbath

1. Slip three washers on the eye bolt, with the largest washer on top. Turn the nut on the bolt just enough to fully thread it.
2. Slip the bottom layer of reinforcement between the top two washers on each screw eye. The screw eyes should be about $21/2″$ in from the circumference and spaced equally around the circle. Wire the eyes in position to the mesh.
3. As you pour the concrete, keep the bolts upright, and check that the nuts stay at the bottom of the form.

Suspend the bath from the chain.

4. With a hacksaw, cut three 25″ chains.
5. Connect one end of each chain to a single S hook. Bend the hook closed with locking pliers set just tight enough to grab the hook (the last part of the closing action gives the most power with this tool). Use several squeezes at ever-tighter settings to close each hook.
6. Connect the three chains to the eye bolts cast in the birdbath using S hooks.
7. Screw the $3/8″$ screw eye into a strong overhanging limb, in a place where kids don't play, and where cats won't have cover to sneak up on your cleanliness-obsessed avian friends.
8. Measure and saw the hanging chain to length and connect it to the screw eye using an S hook.
9. Get a strong friend to help you connect the hanging chain to the S hook already connected to the birdbath.
10. If water leaks through the eye-bolt holes, caulk them tight.

BUTTERFLY HOUSE

Time was, gardeners interested in attracting flying critters thought exclusively of birds. But in the past few years, it's become obvious that butterflies are not only equally comely, but vital for pollinating plants. Depending on their whim, adults and caterpillars may roost in the single-room occupancy hotel described on this page. With luck, they'll even overwinter in your garden. That's good, since butterflies are losing habitat in many parts of the globe.

About the only challenge in making this hotel for friendly invertebrates is cutting the slots that allow butterflies — but not predators — to enter. Start the slots with a $5/16''$ drill, and use a saber saw, coping saw, or router with $1/4''$ straight bit to complete the job.

Mount the finished house about 15″ from the ground, preferably near a mud puddle. (I asked Alex, my wallowsome eight-year-old, to design a puddle for us. He just rolled his eyes.)

■ MATERIALS

One 10′ #3-grade cedar 1×6 (see note page 5)
One $1^1/_2'' \times 2^1/_2''$ hinge and screws
A handful of 6d galvanized siding nails

■ DIRECTIONS

Start the box

1. Saw the back $5^1/_2'' \times 22^3/_8''$ at the longer face, with a 17° bevel on top.
2. Saw both sides, $5^1/_2'' \times 22^1/_8''$ at the longest dimension, and mitered at 17°.
3. Nail through the back to fasten it to the sides, holding the tops flush.

Prepare the front

4. Saw the front: $5^1/_2'' \times 20^3/_8''$ at the longer face, with the top beveled 17°.
5. Draw a horizontal line 2″ from the top on the front of the front piece. Mark the first hole 1″ from the edge on the line. Mark three more holes $1^1/_{16}''$ apart along the line.
6. Repeat at the bottom of the front. Drill a $5/16''$ hole at each mark.
7. Mark the slots by drawing a line connecting each edge of each pair of holes. Cut the slots with the saber saw, coping saw, or router. The finished front

Butterfly House

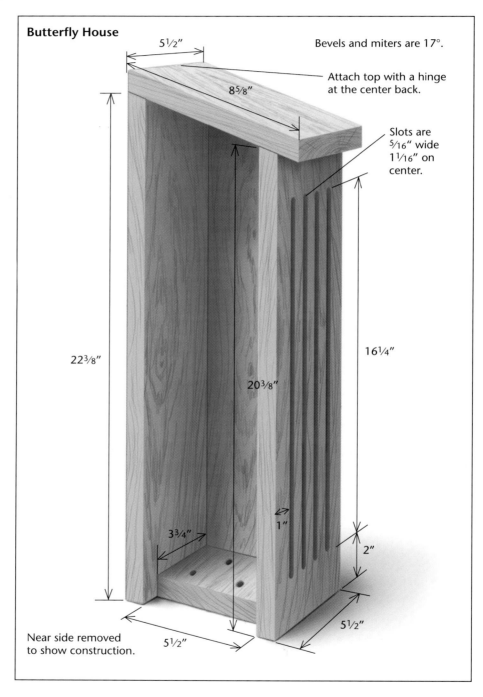

5½"

8⅝"

Bevels and miters are 17°.

Attach top with a hinge at the center back.

Slots are ⁵⁄₁₆" wide 1¹⁄₁₆" on center.

22⅜"

16¼"

20⅜"

1"

3¾"

2"

5½"

5½"

Near side removed to show construction.

should resemble the front view, but don't fret over every last $^1/_{32}''$; last time I checked, butterflies couldn't read calipers.

8. Nail the front into place, with the bottom flush to the sides.

Finish the house

9. Saw the bottom, $3^3/_4'' \times 5^1/_2''$. Drill a few $^1/_8''$ drainage holes, and nail the bottom inside the box.

10. Saw the lid, $5^1/_2'' \times 8^5/_8''$, beveled at both ends.

11. Fasten the hinge to the lid and the back of the box.

12. Mount the completed box about 15″ up a short post, in a sheltered part of the garden. Try to place it in contact with some plants so that your arthropod guests can walk in on a green carpet.

13. Stuff some flowers, leaves, and branches inside the house to make the 'flies feel at home and support their cocoons. It wouldn't hurt to plant some nectar-producing bushes, either, but then that's another Taylor's Guide.

BAT HOUSE

Bats — as everybody knows by now — are not vectors of disease and decay, or signals for dismay and disgust. Instead, they're mammalian insect controls and pollinators — an endangered but essential part of many healthy ecosystems. The following design was developed by Bat Conservation International. BCI (P. O. Box 162603, Austin, TX 78716) will be glad to furnish more than you might want to know about bats or sell you a primo book on bat-house construction, with several more designs, and oodles of suggestions for attracting bats.

Be kind to your airborne mammalian guests: don't paint the inside or use preservative-treated wood. If the interior is too smooth, the bats won't be able to get a foothold. BCI suggests using $^1/_4''$ hardware cloth, or better, a $^1/_8''$ mesh plastic netting, such as product #XV-1670, available from Internet Co. at 800-328-8456. Fasten the netting or hardware cloth with rustproof staples. Keep the house dry by caulking the seams before painting.

Bats prefer a neighborhood with farm fields or orchards, and a lake or stream, but if you've ever been troubled by bats in the belfry (or attic), then you know they're in the neighborhood and you could succeed in attracting them.

Bats like living at least 15′ above the ground, for protection against mammal and snake predators. And they're temperature-sensitive, preferring conditions between 80° and 100°. In the warmest climates, the house will need some shade. Otherwise, put it in a sunny location, like the side of a building, with at least six hours of sun per day. Pay special attention to color, which determines how much solar heat the house will absorb. Remember: keep these little mammals warm!

■ **MATERIALS**

One 10′ 1 × 2
2′ × 8′ × 1/2″ exterior (CDX) plywood
Forty–fifty 1⅝″ deck screws
A few 3″ deck screws for mounting
A handful of galvanized 1″ nails
20″ × 49″ of 1/8″ plastic mesh
One quart latex paint
One tube paintable latex caulk
5/16″ staples
Screws for mounting to tree or building
(For a smaller — 24″ × 26½″ — house, use 2′ × 4′ piece of 1/2″ plywood, and
    one 8′ 1 × 2)

■ **DIRECTIONS**

1. Saw the plywood to 51″ × 24″, 33″ × 24″, and 12″ × 24″. (If your summer is extremely cold, omit the ventilation space and make the front from one piece, 45″ × 24″.)
2. Cut the 1 × 2 to make two 43½″ pieces and one 24″ piece.
3. Lay a bead of caulking on one side of these 1 × 2s.
4. Tack the plywood back to the 1 × 2s, with the 24″ piece running all the way across the top and the 43½″ pieces running below the 24″ piece.
5. Staple the mesh or hardware cloth to the back, making sure it lies flat.
6. Squirt a bead of caulking on the exposed surface of the 1 × 2s, and screw the top front into place. The screws should enter the back plywood.
7. Screw the bottom front into position, leaving a 1/2″ gap for ventilation.
8. Screw through the back into the front plywood pieces.
9. Optional: attach a 4″ × 28″ top.
10. Caulk seams if needed.
11. Paint and screw to tree or building (see above for mounting suggestions).

Bat House

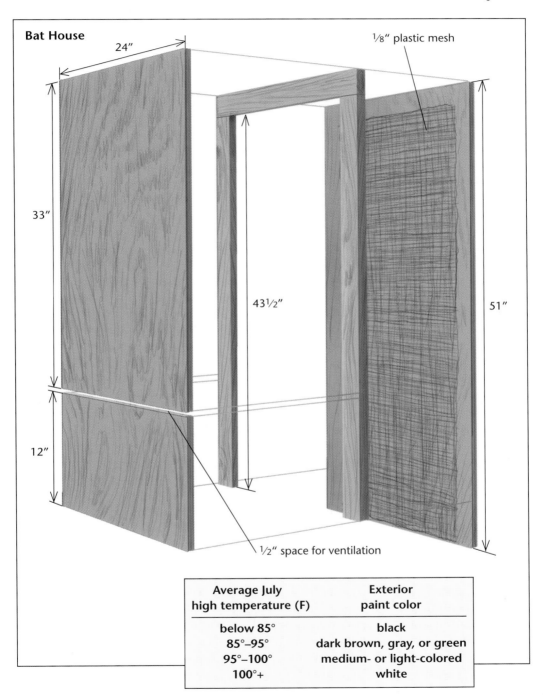

24"

1/8" plastic mesh

33"

43 1/2"

51"

12"

1/2" space for ventilation

Average July high temperature (F)	Exterior paint color
below 85°	black
85°–95°	dark brown, gray, or green
95°–100°	medium- or light-colored
100°+	white

Chapter 4:
Getting Around: Paths, Walls, and Gates

Now we come to the projects that give structure to your garden. Paths promote access here, deny it there, and channel the eye to emphasize prize plantings. Retaining walls help you use hilly slopes and repay your labor by giving a three-dimensional flavor to your garden — not to mention that stone walls offer the opportunity to make a miniature rock garden. And the ornamental gates we describe will help you build a fence that can hide a neighbor's homely garage or conceal your own compost heap.

Paths

As in many garden decisions, paths are a compromise between practicality and aesthetics. The best bet when laying out paths is to notice where people naturally walk, and try to accommodate those routes without overly compromising your aesthetic sense.

Brick pathway: The semi-regularity of these brick steps brings just enough order to this varied plant border.

Traffic levels, climate, budget, and aesthetics will determine your choice of paving material. For occasional use, grass, creeping thyme, or a similar plant may serve. For medium-traffic paths, try stone, mulch, chips, or gravel.

For high-traffic paths, you could use poured concrete, and with the right coloring or surface treatment, it might not even look hideously ugly. But take it from a reformed mason who's poured far too much concrete: this is strictly for masochists. Let's skip concrete in favor of more rewarding materials. I'm thinking of concrete or clay pavers — specially designed units suited to ground contact that often have an interlocking shape that simplifies laying.

Prepare the base

The first step in making a path is to put in stakes to mark the location. If the path does not have the required stable, dry base, fill in low spots so that they're subtly above the surrounding grade.

For a path made of vegetation, "crown" the path so that rain drains not to Spain but to the side, smooth the soil, and plant. Allow a bit of extra height so that when the disturbed soil settles, it remains above the surrounding grade.

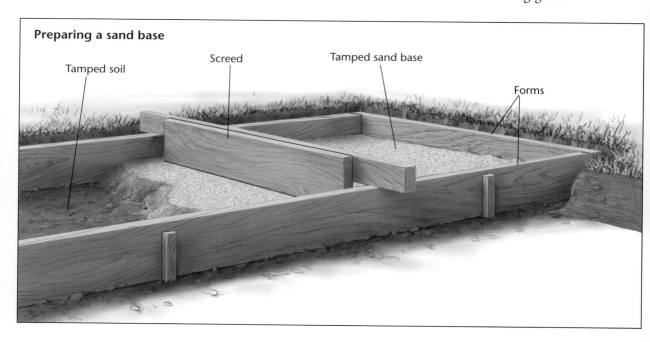

Preparing a sand base

Tamped soil

Screed

Tamped sand base

Forms

For a sand-based path, dig out the path one thickness of the paving material, plus about 3″ for the sand bed. For the strongest base, stake form boards along the edges, and use a screed to level the sand. Then tamp the sand firmly into place, add sand to the low spots, and screed again. Soak the sand with a sprinkler and tamp until the bed is perfectly smooth.

If you're feeling fastidious (you know who you are!), put a layer of weed-barrier cloth on top of the sand. Another material that separates the perfectionists from me and my fellow "it's perfect-enoughers" is edging. Edging keeps the path in its place, and it's pretty easy to do if you plan ahead. You can use bricks set on edge, or use boards or timbers. Landscaping firms sell plastic or steel edging that attaches to small stakes and can be bent into subtle curves.

Bark or Mulch

Cacao shells, wood chips, or shredded bark make a subtle, simple path that shouldn't call attention to itself and definitely won't crack. About the only hang-up is edges — these substances love to stray from the path. Prepare a soil base and edging. Dump about 4″ of your paving material into place and tamp it down. Plan on occasionally adding more mulch as the older stuff packs down.

Gravel

The gravel you use for a path needn't be the boring crushed rock favored by road builders: you can look for bluestone, white stone, or whatever the local landscape-materials specialists happen to have that happens to suit your garden. Like mulch, gravel benefits from edging. Prepare the soil base, lay out the edging, and shovel on a 2″ layer. Rake the gravel smooth, and roll or tamp into position. Then put on another layer, paying special attention to filling low spots in the first layer.

Stone

It's not surprising that stone looks at home in the garden — since stone lives in soil. Unless you're going to use a reinforced concrete base (no weekend project, that!), I strongly suggest not mortaring a path made from stone, brick, or concrete pavers. Instead, opt for the flexibility and error tolerance of a sand base (see above) and dry (mortarless) construction.

Your problem will be finding stone that's strong enough to resist weathering and flaking, while still lending the right feel to the garden. In general, squarer stone is easier to lay, more formal in appearance, and more expensive. Rougher stone suits a more rustic garden, but can be tough to lay accurately and can pose a tripping hazard.

To lay irregular stones in a path, place the stones in position and mark the edges on the ground. Then use a shovel — preferably one you've sharpened with a file — to dig out the outline, a bit deeper than the thickness of the stone. Backfill slightly with sand, nestle the stone into position, and tamp it a few times with a 2 × 4. When done, the stones should be slightly above the surrounding grade.

BRICK AND CONCRETE PAVERS

These ready-made paving units have a key advantage over stone: they're easier to work with, as they're made in rectangles and various interlocking shapes. Any brick used for paving should be a high-fired material designed for the rigors of ground contact. Old bricks may look good at first, but in a couple of years, frost is likely to split them apart. If a brick absorbs water on the surface, it's too porous for ground-contact use.

Using brick or concrete pavers

With all the work you've expended simply placing a sand base (and possibly edging) for your path, you'd think brick or concrete pavers would be kind enough to lay themselves. No such luck. You'll need to do it. Here's how:

Prepare the sand base and forms as detailed above. For complicated or wide paths, you may need to place a string to guide you. Otherwise, use straight boards as guides.

Work from one end and place the pavers in position. Don't slide the units sideways — that traps sand between them. Key point: Never assume; always use a hand level to be sure every paver is level and lined up correctly. Tap each unit into position with the handle of a hammer. Don't let anything get out of place — you'll never be able to correct it.

When everything is finished, throw sand across the path and sweep it into the joints. Soak the path and repeat the process until the joints are full.

Paving Patterns

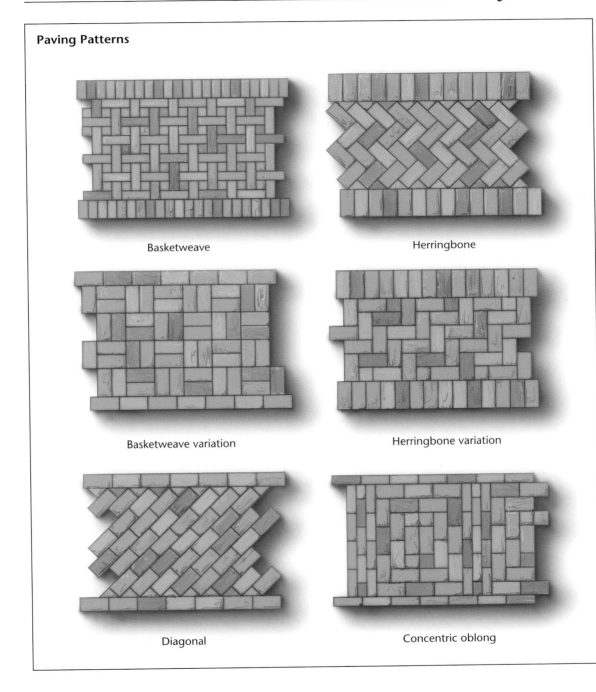

Basketweave

Herringbone

Basketweave variation

Herringbone variation

Diagonal

Concentric oblong

Cutting pavers

Inevitably, no matter what pattern you use, you'll have to cut pavers. The following Neolithic technique will work, but forget about accuracy in hundredths of an inch. It's best to remove a bit more paver than seems necessary.

1. Mark the cut on the paver, and lay it on a bed of sand.
2. Using a 2-lb. hammer and a broad, flat chisel (a "brick set"), gently tap along the cut on all four surfaces of the paver.
3. Swing the hammer harder to finish the cut.

If you can't get the hang of this "Fred Flintstone" routine, cut the pavers with a rented tile or brick saw.

RETAINING WALLS

If your garden has the mixed blessing of a sloping site, you're probably interested in retaining walls. In general, retaining walls need footings, drainage, and an eye-friendly material — meaning stone or wood. Although amateurs should not try building a wall more than two feet high, you can deal with steep grades by cutting them into terraces supported by several low retaining walls.

Stone Retaining Walls

A good stone wall is essentially a pile of stones that were chosen and assembled to exploit gravity. As we saw in the section on raised beds, it's best to build a stone wall "dry," or mortarless, which allows space for drainage and lets the wall move when frost heaves it. The alternative is to build labor-intensive footings, or face endless cracking — or both.

Start the project by marking the wall with string and stakes. If the wall site slopes considerably from side to side, plan on building short, level sections, connected by stair steps — a snaky wall is weak and hard on the eye.

Now dig out a trench that's level from front to back for the gravel footing (the gravel improves drainage and reduces the effects of frost heaving). After tamping the soil, dump in several inches of gravel and rake it smooth.

Flat, broad stones are the easiest to build with, although with some care, rounder ones will work. The first course should consist of the broadest stones, laid flat-side-down. As you build, angle, or "batter," the stones slightly toward the rear so that the wall leans against the soil it is retaining. Overlap stones as much as possible as you lay up the successive courses. This lets gravity bond the courses. Try to avoid stacking vertical joints on top of each other.

To break stones, wear goggles and repeatedly hammer where you want to cut with a brick chisel, a stone hammer, or another bludgeonlike tool. (This el-crudo technique works better than you'd expect.) Keep a pile of gravel available for backfilling the stones, which cramps them into position and promotes drainage.

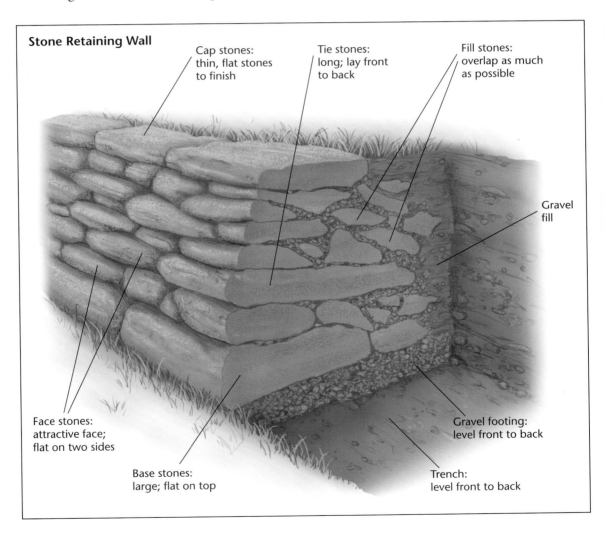

Stone Retaining Wall

Cap stones:
thin, flat stones
to finish

Tie stones:
long; lay front
to back

Fill stones:
overlap as much
as possible

Gravel
fill

Face stones:
attractive face;
flat on two sides

Base stones:
large; flat on top

Gravel footing:
level front to back

Trench:
level front to back

Chink up the bigger gaps in front with stone chips. If you're intending to grow plants in the wall, fill the gaps with soil.

Wood Retaining Walls

Wood makes fast, affordable retaining walls, to a maximum of 18″ to 24″ tall. (Higher walls must be anchored into the hillside with timbers laid horizontally, at right angles to the wall.) The best wood to use is CCA-treated landscape timbers; I'd avoid railroad ties and other wood treated with highly toxic creosote or pentachlorophenol. Wear a dust mask while sawing and drilling CCA-treated wood.

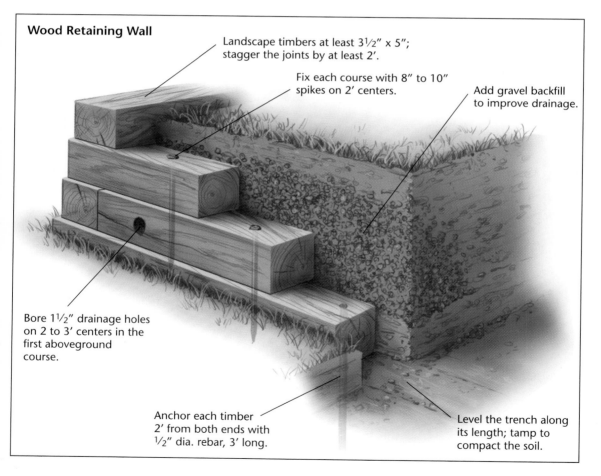

Wood Retaining Wall

Landscape timbers at least 3½″ x 5″; stagger the joints by at least 2′.

Fix each course with 8″ to 10″ spikes on 2′ centers.

Add gravel backfill to improve drainage.

Bore 1½″ drainage holes on 2 to 3′ centers in the first aboveground course.

Anchor each timber 2′ from both ends with ½″ dia. rebar, 3′ long.

Level the trench along its length; tamp to compact the soil.

Lay out the wall with stakes and string. Dig a trench almost as deep as your timbers so that the first course will be stabilized by partial burial. (If your retaining wall will slope from side to side, use the stairstep effect described under Stone Retaining Walls.) Tamp the soil well, and make sure the first course lies flat — the succeeding courses will only amplify any problems at this point. To make sure the first course is in solid contact with the soil, drop the timbers into position, and notice where they impress on the soil. Scalp off these high spots and check again.

When the first course is good and flat, drill $1/2''$ holes in the timbers 2' from each corner and every 6' along straight sections. Pound a 3' piece of $1/2''$ reinforcing rod through each hole to anchor the wall.

Lay the succeeding courses with joints overlapping. Each course should be offset $1/2''$ to 1″ so that the whole wall tilts toward the hillside (the tops of the timbers should stay level). Secure each course with 8″ to 10″ spikes — driven with a big hammer (don't try using your 16-oz. nail hammer). You might want to predrill holes to simplify the spiking. Drill $1^{1}/2''$ drainage holes every 2' to 3' in the first aboveground course. Backfill the wall with gravel for drainage, and fill soil on the uphill side to within 1″ to 2″ of the top.

WATTLE FENCE

As a counterbalance to hideous chain-link and fussy picket fences, nothing could be more welcome than the current vogue for rustic fences. Making a low, wattle fence is an adventure in carpentry without squares, measuring tapes — even nails. In other words, it's fun for the free spirit.

Here are some material and technique guidelines, which apply equally to wattle fences and rustic furniture:

- Yew, apple, and pear were favorites of 18th-century rustic-furniture builders, but hickory, white oak, and ash are all strong, supple woods. Willow, while flexible, is rather weak, so you should make your pieces abnormally thick.
- If you work quickly and neatly, you might be able to scavenge limbs from tree trimmers.
- You'll get the easiest bending from wood that's still green.

- Attach by nailing, screwing, or lashing with vine or cord. See the constrictor knot on page 41 for one good way to tie limbs together. You'll probably have to drill before nailing. Use galvanized nails.
- Concentrate on the overall look, and don't pay obsessive concern to regularity.

To free yourself completely from dimensional anxiety, build your fence in place: position the posts, made from larger-diameter stock, 2′ to 4′ apart, and backfill and tamp well. When the posts are solid, weave the fencing into place. Attach the bottom fence "board" to the near side of a corner post, and fasten its mid-

Wattle fence: *A handmade look and a woven effect combine to make a highly informal but very effective border for low shrubs.*

point to the far side of the next post. Attach the next fence board in the reverse manner, and continue weaving the fence. Work your way along the entire fence so that it forms one unit, not a series of modules.

GATES

Like retaining walls, gates have a hybrid job — part function, part aesthetics. In terms of function, the first requirement is solid corner posts, and that means it's hard to escape the drudgery of digging deep post holes and filling them with concrete. Otherwise, the posts will wander and the gate won't close. Maybe not today. Maybe not tomorrow. But soon. And for the rest of your life.

Hush, Humphrey! We're talking gates, not Ingrid Bergman's love life!

Wide gates are convenient (especially if you're hauling material with a wheelbarrow), so unless space is extremely cramped, make the gate 3′ across. Gates wider than 4′ put a heavy strain on the posts, so you'll have to make them stouter, perhaps from 6 × 6. Wider gates also call for stronger diagonal reinforcement and three big galvanized hinges. Beyond a certain width, it's smarter to build two gates that meet in the middle rather than one monster. It's easiest to build the fence after the gate is in position.

Why describe the construction of gates but not that of fences? Partly, it's because most people buy fencing in ready-made sections — saving time and money. But it's also because even though gates can be a garden focal point, their aesthetic potential is often wasted with contraptions that succeed in excluding the neighbor's Doberman, but fail to grace the garden.

Gates take a beating, so the frame should be pressure-treated lumber; use either rot-resistant cedar or pressure-treated boards for the siding. For better durability, protect the gate from ultraviolet light and moisture with a water-repellent stain. Use screws, not nails, to assemble the frame.

If existing fence posts are sound and plumb (vertical), build the gate to suit them, using the suggestions below, and 1″ narrower than the gap between the posts. This allows 1/4″ clearance between the gate and the hinge post, and 3/4″ clearance to the latch post. Once the gate is completed, prop it 2″ to 3″ above the ground and fasten the hinges, latch, and stop.

If you're building a gate along with a new fence, the best plan is to prefab-

ricate the gate and posts and install them as a unit (assum-
ing they aren't too heavy). This allows you to dodge the usual
struggle of aligning and positioning the gate and posts.

TIPS FOR SUCCESS

For some general
suggestions on using
these plans, see page
113.

Here's how to build and install a gate and posts as a unit:

1. Build a rectangular frame, using either butt or rabbet
   joints, from pressure-treated 2 × 4. Fasten each corner
   with three 3″ rustproof screws. Work on a flat surface so that your gate stays
   flat.

2. Measure the diagonals (which are equal in any rectangle). Now mark and cut
   a diagonal brace from a 2 × 4, mitering only one side of each end. Take care
   not to cut the brace too short — leave your pencil marks visible after sawing. After rechecking that the gate is square, screw the brace into position
   with three 3″ rustproof screws per joint.

3. Attach siding to match or complement your fence (use pickets, solid boards,
   or one of the geometric tops described below) with 8d galvanized siding nails.
   Nail through the siding into the brace and the crossbars.

4. Attach hinges to the framing with 2″ rustproof screws. Place the hinge pin
   overhanging the gate.

5. Cut the posts long enough to insert at least 3′ (up to 4′ in cold climates)
   into the ground. The gate should clear the ground by 2″ to 3″.

6. Visualize the direction the gate will swing, then screw the hinges to the gate
   post, allowing 1/4″ clearance between gate and post.

7. Nail a 1 × 4 stop to the latch post (on the side away from the hinges) to prevent the gate from overswinging and wrecking the hinges. Then tack-nail the
   stop to the gate, allowing 3/4″ clearance. This step ensures that the gate and
   the posts stay aligned while you install the posts.

8. Attach the latch.

9. Dig two holes at least 40″ deep, add 4″ of gravel, and position the gate and
   posts in the hole. Rest the gate on wood blocks to get the desired ground
   clearance.

10. Brace each post in the vertical position with two braces, and fill the post
    holes with concrete. Round off the top, making a concrete collar for drainage.

11. When the concrete is set, remove the nails tacking the gate to the stop.

Gate

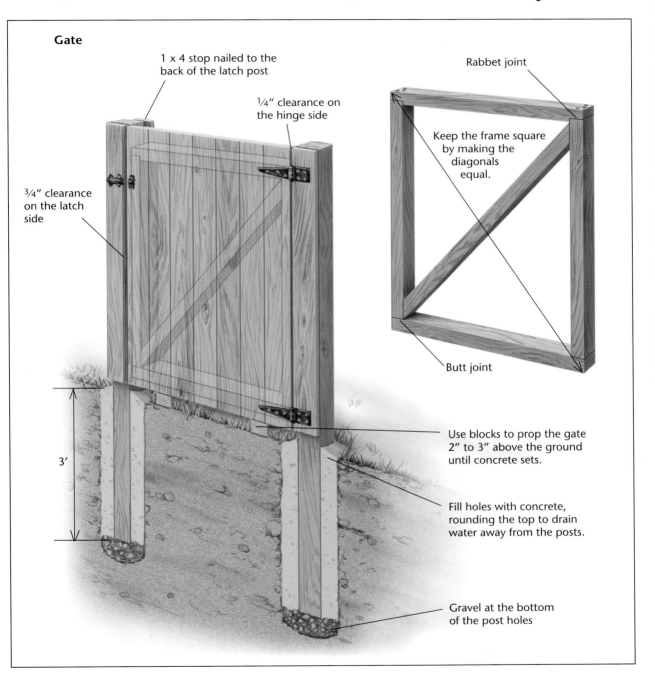

1 x 4 stop nailed to the back of the latch post

¼" clearance on the hinge side

Rabbet joint

Keep the frame square by making the diagonals equal.

¾" clearance on the latch side

Butt joint

Use blocks to prop the gate 2" to 3" above the ground until concrete sets.

3'

Fill holes with concrete, rounding the top to drain water away from the posts.

Gravel at the bottom of the post holes

ARCHED GATE TOPS

A gate needn't be a mere continuation of a boring fence — it can also have architectural interest of its own. Here are some arch designs that, although easy to draw, have a certain classic elegance. Use a pencil on a string for the overgrown divider these arches require.

Each arch begins with this basic procedure.

1. On a sheet of cardboard wider than the gate and at least 3′ in the other dimension, draw line AB across the bottom. Length AB equals the gate width.

2. Draw line CD at the center of AB, and perpendicular to it. Now skip to the directions for whichever arch you prefer. When you're finished, cut the cardboard to make a template for the gate top.

Segmental arch

3. Extend line CD below line AB and mark point E some distance below point C.

4. Using a divider set to length AE, draw the arch. If you don't like the shape, move point E and try again.

Elliptical arch

3. Mark point E on line CD $^2/_5$ the gate width above line AB.

4. Mark points F and G at length CA away from point E on line AB.

5. Place the cardboard on a scrap of wood, and drive nails into points F and G. Tie a loop of string around these nails long enough to include point E.

6. Place a pencil in the loop. Leave the loop around the nails, and draw the arch while holding the loop taut.

Gothic arch

3. Decide how tall you want the arch, and mark it as point E on line CD.

4. Draw straight line AE and mark its middle as point F.

5. Draw line FG perpendicular to AE.

6. From point G, with radius AG, draw the right half of the arch.

7. Repeat steps 4 through 6 to draw the left half.

Templates for Arched Gate Tops

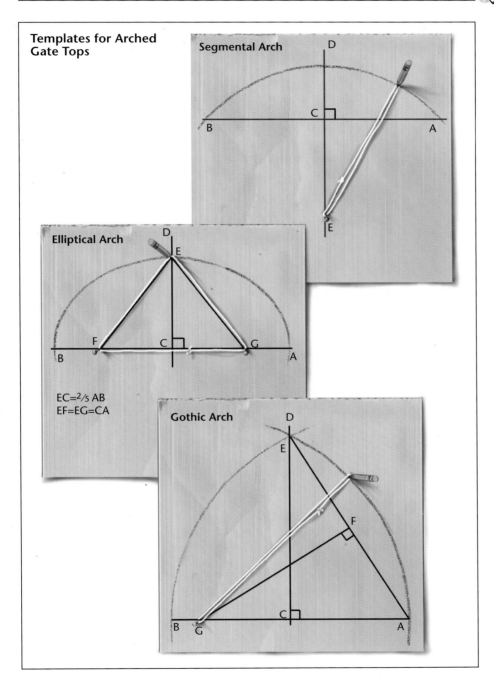

Segmental Arch

Elliptical Arch

EC=²/₅ AB
EF=EG=CA

Gothic Arch

CHAPTER 5:

FROM PRACTICAL TO FANCIFUL

Believe it or not, there actually are gardeners who take the time to relax amidst their creations. Granted, it's usually on a hot summer day when there's not another weed to be pulled and the seedlings have all grown up or died. If you are one of these favored few, then there's no place more satisfying to do that relaxing than on a wooden bench of your own manufacture. If your garden is blessed with a big shade tree in a central location, you can make a tree bench as a garden focus.

If relaxing in midsummer sounds like less fun than building, you could always wax utilitarian by building a wooden doormat with a geometric design, a little house for your trash can, or a sandbox for the kids. For the artistically inclined, we've included suggestions for the ultimate garden decoration — heroic-scale sculptures of concrete decorated with broken glass.

Pioneer farmers relied on picks and muscle-power to dig stumps from their fields. This is one of roughly 200 sculptures built by retired farmer, logger, and barkeep Fred Smith in his backyard along Highway 13 south of Phillips, Wisconsin. His legacy, the Wisconsin Concrete Park, is free, public, and divinely cool.

WOOD FREESTANDING BENCH OR TABLE

A garden bench — should it be ornate, rococo, or Shaker-plain? I chose the latter, partly because it fits my garden, mainly because it suits my woodworking skills. This bench is 42″ long by 14″ wide; as usual, you can alter the specifications to meet your needs. To make a table, just skip steps 12–15, where you would shape the crossbars so that the bench seat fits the basal human anatomy.

You'll need a table saw or circular saw, a saber saw or coping saw, and a variable-speed drill (for countersinking and screwing). For comfort's sake, slightly round the corners of all top boards with a plane, and then smooth them with sandpaper.

■ MATERIALS

#3-grade cedar: one 8′ 1 × 6, one 8′ 1 × 8
One 10′ cedar 2 × 4
Rustproof deck screws: two $1^1/_4$″, sixteen each 2″ and 3″
$^1/_4$ lb. 8d galvanized siding nails
Two sheets each, medium and fine sandpaper

> **TIPS FOR SUCCESS**
>
> For some general suggestions on using these plans, see page 113.

■ DIRECTIONS

Make the leg assemblies

1. From 2 × 4, cut four legs $1^1/_2$″ × $1^{11}/_{16}$″ × $15^1/_2$″, mitered at the top 9° across the $1^{11}/_{16}$″ face.
2. Saw the front and rear rails $1^1/_2$″ × $2^1/_2$″ × 31″. Set the rails aside for step 7.
3. From the remainder from step 2, saw four leg end braces, $^3/_4$″ × $^3/_4$″ × 12″, with 45° miters on both ends.
4. Tack through two scraps of wood into the ends of a pair of legs to make a temporary box with:
    a) the legs parallel and $11^3/_8$″ apart (outside measurement),
    b) the $1^{11}/_{16}$″ faces up, and
    c) the mitered ends as shown.
5. Fasten the leg end braces diagonally with one 2″ countersunk screw per joint, with the bottom of the braces $2^1/_2$″ above floor level. Fasten the intersection between the braces with a 1 $^1/_4$″ screw. Remove the scrap pieces.
6. Repeat steps 4 and 5 for the other pair of legs.

Wood Freestanding Bench or Table

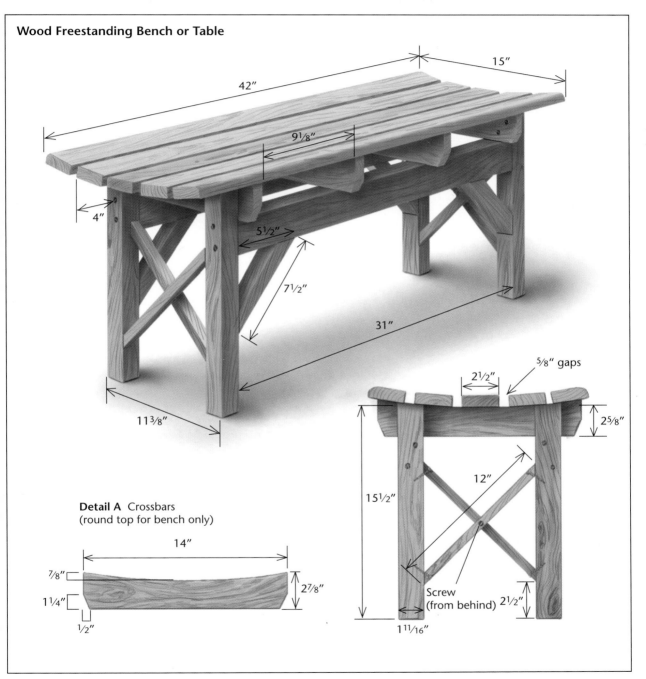

42"

15"

9⅛"

4"

5½"

7½"

31"

11⅜"

⅝" gaps

2½"

2⅝"

12"

15½"

Screw
(from behind) 2½"

1¹¹⁄₁₆"

Detail A Crossbars
(round top for bench only)

14"

⅞"

1¼"

½"

2⅞"

Finish the frame

7. Screw the leg assemblies to the ends of the rails you made in step 2, using two countersunk 3″ deck screws per joint. The tops of the rails are $2^5/8$″ below the tops of the legs. Place the legs with the $1^1/4$″ screws facing inside.

8. From a 16″ length of 2 × 4, rip two pieces $1^1/4$″ × $1^1/2$″ for the front and back leg braces. Miter both ends at 45° to make four pieces $7^1/2$″ long by $1^1/4$″ thick (from front to back).

9. Screw these braces to the legs and rails with one 2″ countersunk screw per joint.

Make and fasten the crossbars

10. From the 1 × 8, saw two pieces 14″ long. Then rip these to make four crossbars $2^7/8$″ wide. Save the remainder for seat boards (step 18).

11. Miter the bottom corners of the crossbars as shown in detail A.

12. On one crossbar, mark the center of the curve at $7/8$″ from one edge (see detail A). (To make a table instead of a bench, skip steps 12–15).

13. Draw the curve freehand. Start with a light line, and refine it as you go.

14. Cut this piece with the saber saw or coping saw. Use it as a template to mark and saw the cuts on the other three crossbars.

15. Stack the crossbars and round off the curves with a rasp so they're similar. (Don't use a micrometer — this is not for the queen's parlor!)

16. Fasten the crossbars to the front and rear rails with one deeply countersunk 3″ screw per joint. Screw vertically through the crossbar into the rail. Important: don't place screws between 2″ and 3″ from the end of the crossbars, as these screws would be visible after the seat boards are attached).

17. Screw the end crossbars to the legs with two 2″ screws per joint. Place the screws low on the crossbars.

Fasten the seat boards

18. Rip five pieces $2^1/2$″ × 42″ for the seat boards.

19. Plane the cut edges and lightly round the top corners. Plane (or round with a router) the outside edge of the front and back seat boards. Sandpaper all seat boards.

20. Fasten the seat boards, about $5/8$″ apart, and $1/2$″ overhanging the ends of the crossbars, with two 8d galvanized siding nails per joint. Take care not to nail into the screws holding the crossbars.

TREE BENCH

Here's my interpretation of those wonderful benches built around trees. These garden classics are oddly absent from most backyard project books — perhaps because trees come in a lot of sizes. I've evaded that problem by showing you how to design a bench for any size tree.

A complete bench needs six seat modules, but you can make one with three or four to go partway around a tree. The four $3^{1}/_{2}''$-wide bench boards, spaced $^{1}/_{2}''$ apart, give a total bench depth of $15^{1}/_{2}''$ from front to back.

You can build a backrest, again in modules, but I'll leave that bit of Euclidean brainstorming to you — with the warning that it might call for the dreaded compound-miter saw cuts.

You'll need a large sheet of cardboard for the layout. You'll also need large dividers (compass), or a string and pencil. A table saw and a countersink for your drill would also be quite handy.

Since I don't know the diameter of your tree, I left the material calculations to you and have only listed the varieties of wood you'll need. The hardware listed should be enough for a complete, six-module bench.

■ MATERIALS

Pressure-treated 2 × 4 for radial framing, legs, and horizontal leg braces (or substitute cedar, which will be weaker but better-looking)

#3-grade cedar 1 × 4 for bench top and leg angle braces

About one lb. 6d galvanized box or siding nails

Twenty-four $1^{5}/_{8}''$ and forty-eight $2^{1}/_{2}''$ deck screws

Twelve 1″-thick paving bricks or blocks for supporting the legs

■ DIRECTIONS

Lay out the seat module

1. Measure the diameter of your tree along its broadest dimension. Divide this by 2, then add at least 3″ for growing room. This is the inside radius length AB.

2. Mark point A on a large piece of cardboard, and draw a quarter circle using the inside radius (see layout guide).

3. With the divider still set at the inside radius, mark point B on the left side of the cardboard. Mark point C one inside radius away from B. Both points are on the original arc. Draw straight line BC.

4. Draw a line parallel to BC and 15½″ farther from the center.

5. Draw lines from A through points B and C to locate points D and E on the parallel line. BCDE is the outline of one seat module, seen from above, and represents one-sixth of a full bench.

Make the frame and legs

6. If you don't have a table saw, make a cardboard template with a 120° end angle for marking end cuts on the radial framing.

7. Using the template if needed, saw two pieces of radial framing from 2 × 4, laid flat. Measured along the centerline, these pieces are ³⁄₄″ shorter than length BE. Mark the centerline on each radial framing piece.

8. Saw four legs from 2 × 4. Legs 12½″ long give a low-to-the-ground bench that I found pleasing (the bench top will be 2³⁄₈″ above the leg tops). Make longer legs if you prefer a tall perch.

9. Bevel the front of the front legs twice with the saw set at 30° so that, when looking from above, they have the same angle as the end of the radial framing.

10. Screw the legs into position through the top of a radial framing piece using two countersunk 2½″ screws per leg. The rear of the rear legs touch the back of the radial framing; the front of the front legs are ³⁄₄″ recessed from the front of the radial framing.

11. Saw the leg angle braces from ⁷⁄₈″ × ⁷⁄₈″ material mitered 30° at the ends. Holding the legs square to the radial framing and the mitered ends of the braces out, use one 1⁵⁄₈″ screw per joint. Important: Leave room for the horizontal leg braces in step 16.

Assemble the seat module

12. Miter seat board one from 1 × 4 so that its shorter dimension equals BC. Round the edges (but not the ends) slightly on all seat boards, and sand them before installing.

13. Miter seat board two 30° at both ends, with the longer dimension equaling DE. Round the front of the board with a router or plane.

14. Carefully fasten these boards to the radial framing with two 6d nails per end. Pay attention to the angles so that the mitered ends meet the centerlines you drew on the radial framing. Boards one and two should be parallel and 8½″ apart, with board two overhanging the ends of the radial framing.

Tree Bench

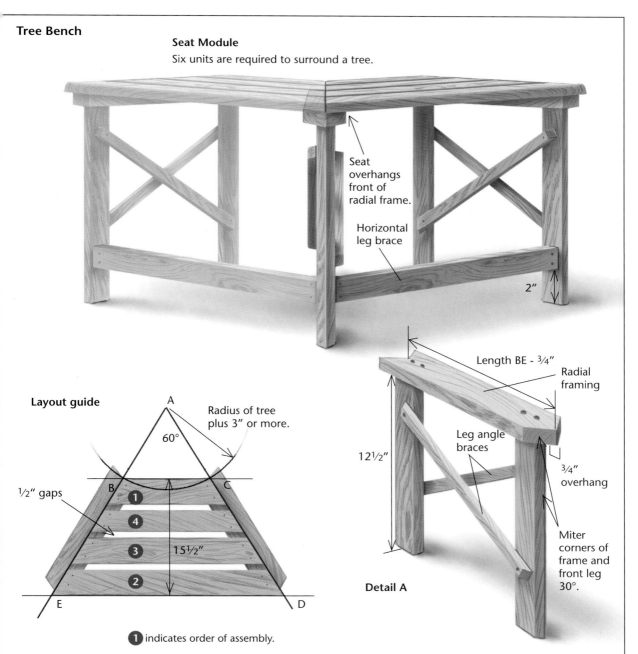

Seat Module
Six units are required to surround a tree.

Seat overhangs front of radial frame.

Horizontal leg brace

2"

Layout guide

A

Radius of tree plus 3" or more.

60°

½" gaps

B

C

① ④ ③ ②

15½"

E

D

① indicates order of assembly.

Length BE - ¾"

Radial framing

12½"

Leg angle braces

¾" overhang

Miter corners of frame and front leg 30°.

Detail A

15. Miter boards three and four so that they extend exactly to the centerlines on the two radial framing pieces and are spaced $1/2''$ apart. Nail them into position.

16. Make a horizontal leg brace from $1^1/2'' \times 1^1/2''$ material with a 30° miter at each end. The brace should be flush to the back of the front legs and 2″ up from the bottom. Screw through the legs with two $2^1/2''$ screws per joint.

17. Make as many more modules as you need. Assemble them around the tree, and nail the seat boards into position. If your bench will not completely encircle the tree, extend the seat boards on the end modules $1^1/2''$ beyond the radial framing and round them off.

18. Prop the legs on pavers so that they rest evenly.

WOODEN DOORMAT

Has your welcome mat worn out its welcome? If so, here's a wooden replacement that's sure to please. If you don't have a table saw, you may be able to pay a lumber yard (or beg a friend) to cut the rippings for you; after that, a hand miter box would suffice for the cutting. You'll need a countersink for the screws.

Take your time with this project, and don't work too far ahead of yourself. Since minor errors in positioning can add up, we'll use a spacer to make sure everything stays on target. And anyway it's kosher to adjust the spacing of pieces if something goes wrong, so long as you do so gradually. Pay close attention to the suggested nailing order — otherwise you won't be able to assemble the mat.

■ MATERIALS

#3-grade cedar (see note page 5): one 6′ 1 × 8 and one 3′ 1 × 6 (this supplies extra wood so that you can trash the weak pieces with weirdo knots)

Rustproof deck screws: four each $1^1/2''$ and 3″

One lb. 8d galvanized siding nails (Kids: Do not try this trick with thicker nails — you're sure to split the wood!)

Wooden Doormat

Slats are all ⅞" x ⅞". Lengths shown.

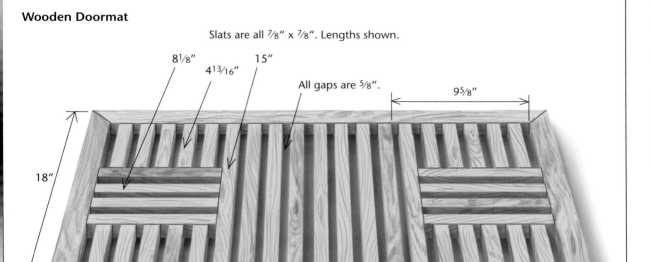

8⅛"
4¹³/₁₆"
15"
All gaps are ⅝".
9⅝"
18"
29⅛"
32⅛"

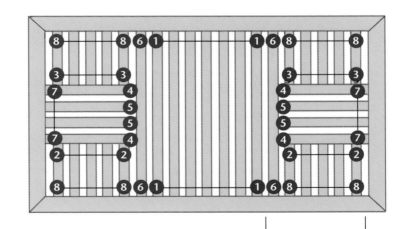

Nailing order for assembling the slats

Assemble this section after completing the rest of the doormat.

1 indicates order of assembly.

■ DIRECTIONS

Build the frame

1. Rip a 36″ 1 × 6 to make three pieces, $1\frac{1}{2}$″ wide.
2. Miter these pieces at 45° to make two pieces 18″ long and two pieces $32\frac{1}{8}$″.
3. Holding the frame square, countersink two holes at each end of each shorter frame piece, and screw the frame together with one screw of each size per joint.

Make the middle innards

4. Rip a spacer exactly $\frac{5}{8}$″ wide, and use it to position the inside pieces in the following steps.
5. From now on, all rippings will be $\frac{7}{8}$″ × $\frac{7}{8}$″. Cut nine rippings 15″ long and put two aside.
6. Nail seven 15″ pieces at nailing site #1, starting $9\frac{5}{8}$″ from the inside of one end. Nail through the outside of the frame, using your $\frac{5}{8}$″ spacer to fasten the pieces $1\frac{1}{2}$″ on center. Keep the joints square, make sure the nails don't poke through, and hold the surfaces flush.

Assemble the ends

7. Cut eight rippings $8\frac{1}{8}$″ long. Set four aside.
8. Saw twenty rippings $4\frac{13}{16}$″ long and set ten aside.
9. Nail five $4\frac{13}{16}$″ rippings to one of the $8\frac{1}{8}$″ pieces (from step 7), at nailing site #2. Repeat this step at nailing site #3.
10. Nail these assemblies to an unused 15″ ripping at site #4.
11. Nail two more $8\frac{1}{8}$″ pieces at site #5.
12. Nail the 15″ ripping to the frame at site #6. Make sure everything is square, and keep the joints tight as you nail.
13. Finish the end by nailing at sites #7 and #8, paying attention to spacing and angles, and holding surfaces flush.
14. Repeat steps 9 through 13 to complete the other end, using the rippings you've set aside.
15. Treat with water-repellent stain or other wood preservative for long life.

HOSE GUIDE

To keep your hose out of your flower beds, buy a newel post made for outdoor railings at a lumber yard. These globular decorations come in several shapes; to my eye, the simpler designs are definitely better.

Sharpen a 15″ 2 × 2 with a saw or an ax, and pound it into place until it's about flush with the soil surface. Then drill a hole down into the post and screw the newel into place. What could be simpler?

GARBAGE-CAN HOUSE

If your house is like mine, you've got a problem, and it's called garbage. The garage is too valuable to convert into a garbage dump, and the side of the house is homely enough without becoming a display for the trash can. Short of buying into a daily trash-hauling service, what's a homeowner to do?

Build a little home for your can, that's what. The design shown is 29″ wide × 28″ deep × 38″ high, suitable for most 32-gallon trash cans. It fills from the top, but you can open the front door to lug out the can on trash night. In other words, it's perfect for U.S. Senators — no heavy lifting required.

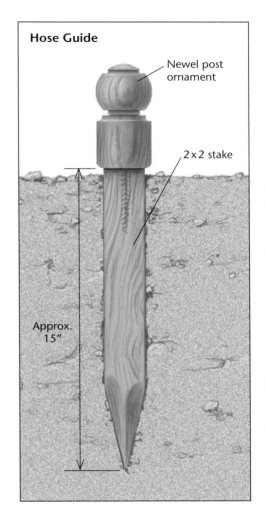

Hose Guide

Newel post ornament

2 x 2 stake

Approx. 15″

Alterations

The garbage-can house is designed to rest on top of the ground; if you're building on dirt, you could sink part of it underground, leaving less to meet the eye (but forcing you to do more lifting on trash night). If that's your style, build the subterranean portion from 4″ × 8″ × 16″ solid concrete blocks — mortar not required. To house two or more trash cans, build the houses in modules.

If your garbage can with lid measures taller than 33″, increase the height of the house accordingly. If you want to add a little recycling bin to the side, use the same 15° angle for its lid.

For this project, you'll need a circular saw, a variable-speed drill with Phillips bit, and a carpenter's or small aluminum square. An adjustable angle square would be handy. The roof slopes at 15°; if you don't have an adjustable square, use a protractor to make a cardboard template for marking the cuts on the 2 × 4s.

■ MATERIALS

Pressure-treated 2 × 4s: two 10′, one 8′
Twenty-one 1 × 4 × 6 #3-grade cedar (see note page 5)
$1/4$″ plywood, 36 × $26 1/2$, for the back
Fourteen truss plates $3 1/8$″ × 7″
One pair spring hinges 3″ × 3″
One pair tee hinges $3 1/2$″ × 5″
One gate latch (the kind that closes when the latch bar snaps into place and opens by raising a small lever)
One lb. $1 5/8$″ rustproof deck screws
A handful of 16d ($3 1/4$″) galvanized nails
One lb. $1 1/2$″ galvanized truss nails
$1/2$ lb. $2 1/4$″ galvanized siding nails
Exterior stain or water-repellent preservative (optional)

■ DIRECTIONS

Build the frame

1. Saw four pieces of 2 × 4 $26 1/2$″ long for the bottom frame. Using two 16d nails per corner, nail up the bottom frame. The bottom side rails rest on edge, while the front and back bottom rails lie flat.
2. Saw two back uprights at $27 3/4$″, mitered 15° at the top.
3. Saw two front uprights at $21 7/8$″, mitered 15° at the top.
4. Using four truss nails per plate, nail two truss plates to the bottom of each of these four uprights. The plates extend $3 1/4$″ inches below the upright.
5. Saw two top side rails to $27 3/8$″, with both ends mitered.
6. Fasten one top side rail on edge atop the uprights:

Garbage-Can House

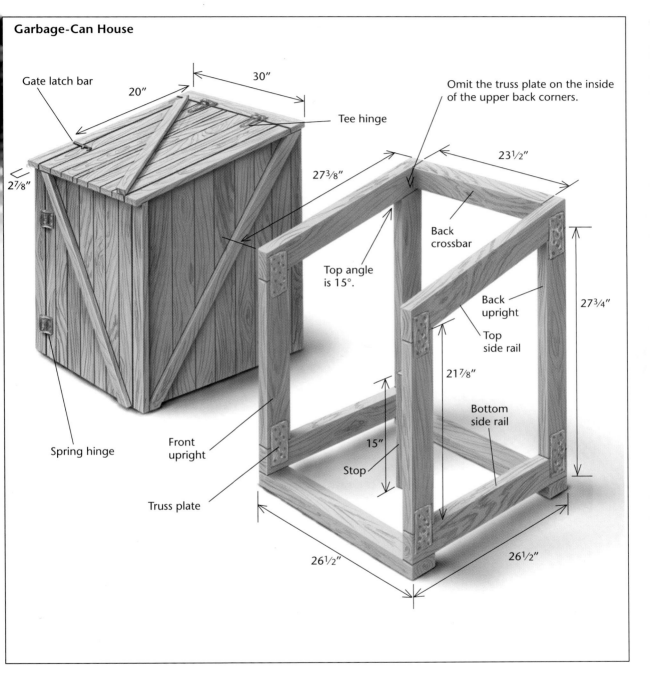

Gate latch bar

20"

30"

Tee hinge

$2^7/8$"

Omit the truss plate on the inside of the upper back corners.

$27^3/8$"

$23^1/2$"

Back crossbar

Top angle is 15°.

Back upright

Top side rail

$27^3/4$"

$21^7/8$"

Bottom side rail

15"

Stop

Spring hinge

Front upright

Truss plate

$26^1/2$"

$26^1/2$"

a) Tack the rail to a front upright with two truss plates. Don't let the truss plates protrude beyond the wood.

b) Tack the rail to a rear upright using one truss plate, on the outside.

c) When the front and back uprights are parallel and at 75° or 105° to the top rail, finish nailing the truss plates.

7. Slip the side frame on the bottom side rail, and tack it with one nail per truss plate.

8. Using a carpenter's square, square up the side frame. Tack a scrap 1 × 4 diagonally to hold the side frame in position. As you finish nailing the truss plates, hold a second hammer behind the 2 × 4 to absorb the shock. This makes a tight joint.

9. Repeat steps 6 to 8 for the second side frame.

10. Saw a 2 × 4 to $23^1/_2$" for the back crossbar:

a) Bevel the rear edge 15° so that the wider face is $2^3/_8$" wide.

b) Nail on edge across the back, flush with the top and back of the side frames.

Make the back

11. Cut the plywood back 36" high × $26^1/_2$" wide.

12. After making sure the box is square, fasten the back by nailing or screwing every 8" into the rear uprights and back bottom rail. Screw every 4" into the top crossbar. Stagger these screws.

Attach the siding

13. Rotate the frame so that the left side is up. Tack a nail $^1/_2$" above ground level on the end of the front and back bottom rails. Stretch a string between the nails to mark the bottom of the siding, which is $^1/_2$" above the ground (to keep the boards dry).

14. Starting at the front, screw seven pieces of 6′ 1 × 4 with the butt edges almost touching the string. Use two $1^5/_8$" screws at each joint, staggered and slightly countersunk.

15. Rip the last board so that it is wide enough to conceal the plywood back, and fasten it.

16. Cut the top of all the siding in one step, flush to the top of the side rail.

17. Turn the frame so that the right-hand side is up. Screw the cutoffs from step

Garbage-Can House

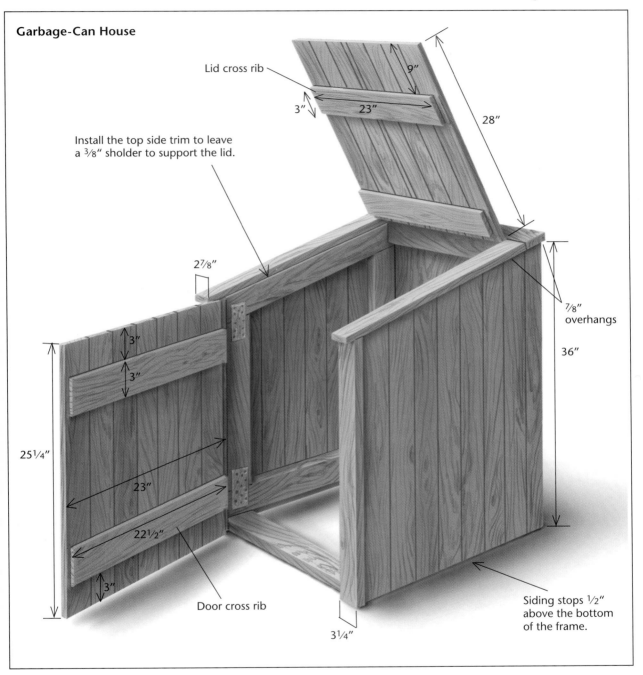

Lid cross rib

9"

3"

23"

28"

Install the top side trim to leave a 3/8" sholder to support the lid.

2 7/8"

7/8" overhangs

36"

3"

3"

25 1/4"

23"

22 1/2"

3"

Door cross rib

3 1/4"

Siding stops 1/2" above the bottom of the frame.

16 with the mitered ends up, flush to the top side rails. Cut off the bottoms
$1/2''$ above ground level.

Make the front

18. Tip the frame on its back. Cut nine 1 × 4s to 30″, and rip two of them to
    $3^1/4''$ for the front trim boards. Screw these to the front corners. They should
    be taller than the side siding; you will cut the tops in step 22. The trim
    boards should be
    a) flush with the inside of the side uprights;
    b) overhanging the side siding by $7/8''$; and
    c) ending $1/2''$ above ground level (the same as the sides).

19. Saw two door cross ribs 1″ × 3″ × $22^1/2''$. Tack four scraps to the front
    uprights, $1^3/4''$ behind the front trim boards. Rest the door cross ribs on these
    scraps.

20. Screw one 30″ 1 × 4 to the cross ribs at each side of the door, allowing $1/8''$
    clearance so that the door can swing. Use two screws per joint. Continue
    screwing the door siding in place, working toward the middle. Ripsaw the
    last board to size and fasten.

21. Screw the spring hinges into place.

22. Mark a line across the top of the door and the front trim boards. Bevel on
    this line at 15° so that the front is flush with the side rails. Remove the scraps
    from step 19 to complete the front.

Make the top

23. Stand the frame upright and saw a 1 × 4 × 30 for the back trim board. Place
    this board from side to side at the back. The trim board should be
    a) overhanging the siding at both sides by $7/8''$, and
    b) have the front even with the front of the back crossbar. Bevel the rear edge
       at 15° to make it flush with the plywood back. Nail into position.

24. Now you will build the top and lid much as you did the front and door. Saw
    nine 28″ 1 × 4s.

25. Rip two of these 28″ pieces to $2^7/8''$ for the top side trim boards. Nail the
    top side trim boards on top of the side rails. The trim board should be
    a) butting against the back trim board;
    b) overhanging the side siding by $7/8''$; and

c) leaving $3/8''$ of the side rail exposed to support the lid.

The lower ends of these boards should be too long; you'll cut them in step 30.

26. Saw two 1 × 3s to 23" for the lid cross ribs. Tack scraps to the top side rails (as in step 19), and rest the cross ribs on the scraps. The top of the upper rib should be $1/2''$ from the top of the lid; the bottom of the lower rib should be $7^1/4''$ behind the front of the frame.

27. Make the sides of the lid by fastening two 28" 1 × 4s (from step 24) to the cross ribs, leaving $1/8''$ clearance at the top and sides.

28. Fasten these pieces to the cross ribs with two screws per joint. Screw the rest of the lid boards in position, working toward the middle. Rip the center board to fit and fasten it.

29. Place the tee hinges as shown and screw into position. Use $1^5/8''$ screws where they will grab the upper cross rib and the back crossbar.

30. Mark a line across the front edge of the lid so that the lid will overhang the front siding by $7/8''$. Bevel all the way across at 15°, making a vertical edge.

Finish up

31. Ripsaw three $1'' \times 7/8'' \times 48''$ angle braces for the two sides and the lid. Hold in position as shown, and mark the mitered end cuts.

32. Miter the ends, return the braces to position, and screw from the inside, using one screw per siding board.

33. Saw a 15" $3/4'' \times 3/4''$ stop for the front door and screw into the side upright that's opposite the hinges so that the door stops closing flush to the front.

34. Position the gate latch bar as shown, and screw into position with screws long enough to grab the lid cross rib.

35. If you will place the structure next to a building, fasten the gate latch to the building where it will catch the latch bar. Or screw a vertical 2 × 2 through the back into the rear side rail, and screw the gate latch to it.

36. Optional: Stain or coat with water-repellent preservative for longer life (stain also helps hide the screw heads, which I find distinctly homely).

SANDBOX

Kids needing some kicks? Maybe it's time to build the ultimate nonbattery, non-video entertainment gizmo — a sandbox. I've shown one that's 6′ × 6′, although

my boys, Alex and Josh, have squeaked by on a 4′ × 5′ model in our small back-yard. You can go bigger, but before you build your kids a backyard Tara, remember that a jumbo sandbox calls for more sand, and that means mucho schlepping. Ouch! Hand tools will work fine on this project, although it would be handy to have a variable-speed drill and a countersink. Please be sure to sandpaper the rough edges so that your kids don't get splinters.

■ MATERIALS

For a 6′ × 6′ sandbox:

Two 12′ 2 × 10s, one 5′ 2 × 6 (I used pressure-treated wood, but if you're nervous about toxicity problems, you could use untreated lumber — just don't expect it to last forever).

Twenty-eight 3″ deck screws

54 cubic feet builder's or mason's sand (or ¾ cubic foot per square foot of sandbox area). Don't emulate my dad, Frank, who robbed sand for our box from

Sandbox

28½″

72″

20½″

Jones Beach, and don't buy bagged sand until you check a masonry supplier, where sand is almost — dare we say it — dirt cheap? Your best bet may be getting the sand delivered — it's about as light as rock.

- **DIRECTIONS**

1. Level the ground and remove obstructions.
2. Saw four 72" 2 × 10s (if your lumber is $^1/_8$" short, don't worry about it). Screw the frame together, using four 3" screws per corner to make a sandbox that's 73 $^1/_2$" square on the outside. Countersink the screws so that they get a good "purchase" on the wood.
3. Saw two 2 × 6s to 28$^1/_2$" for the angle braces, with 45° miters on both ends.
4. Hold the braces in position, and screw them using three screws per joint.
5. Fill the box relatively full of sand. If your kids are anything like mine, the sand will start disappearing immediately. Now pack up your tools and go join them in the sand.

Sandbox: Angle braces give sidewalk supervisors a place to rest while advising the young builders.

BACKYARD SCULPTURE FROM EMBELLISHED CONCRETE

Fred Smith was a retired Wisconsin logger who loathed machines, loved to work with concrete and broken glass, and didn't give much of a hang what anybody thought. In 1950, when the 65-year-old began his prodigious sculpting career, the terms "outsider art" or "grassroots art" were yet to be coined. Thanks in part to artists like Smith, it has become an accepted, if eccentric, artistic tradition that includes work in wood, glass, metal, and concrete. The best-known representative of the genre is Simon Rodia's Watts Towers.

Smith's contribution to what we might call the "unschooled school" was an acre of outdoor sculptures built in his backyard near Phillips, Wisconsin. His first sculpture, an unremarkable stone planter, sparked his interest in building larger-than-life portrayals of North Woods archetypes. Over the course of the next 15

Fred Smith's "stump farmer" is decorated with glass power-line insulators; note the horse's mane, made of upended beer bottles from Smith's tavern. Before they could plant crops, stump farmers faced the backbreaking task of removing thousands of tree stumps.

The crown on Smith's kerosene delivery driver is a glass globe scavenged from an antique gasoline pump.

years, Smith populated what he called Wisconsin Concrete Park with more than 200 loggers, milkmaids, farmers, deer, horse-teams, even Paul Bunyan and his blue ox, Babe. Smith's peculiar outdoor art gallery was part folk history, part personal vision, and all ode to muscle power: not a single machine aids the dozens of grim, determined loggers and farmers.

Unschooled artists like Smith and hundreds of others have discovered something that might benefit the rest of us: you don't need the approval of the "art establishment" to satisfy your inner urgings. You don't need "art supplies" to be an artist. And you don't need a diploma to be expressive: Smith, for example, never attended art school — or any other kind of school for that matter.

If you've got enough energy and imagination, you can satisfy your expressive cravings with ornamented concrete. Although some of the old-timers cast their

A wishing-well planter made by farmer and fiddler Herman Rusch. Rusch's Prairie Moon Museum and Sculpture Garden, near Cochrane, Wisconsin, was recently restored.

This arcaded fence, built in the Mississippi River bottomland by Rusch, is a triumph of amateur backyard building that subtly echoes the landscape.

sculptures in holes in the ground, the armature technique described below will give you much more artistic liberty while allowing you to skip the mold-making process. Instead of giving a detailed procedure, I've listed some pointers to get you started. This is not rocket science. There are no micron tolerances. The mortar recipe and many other suggestions are courtesy of Lisa Stone, a Wisconsin sculptor and conservator at Concrete Park.

Guidelines:

1. Make a sturdy foundation. If you're building for posterity, set a footing below the frost line — which can be as much as 48″ below grade.

2. Make the "armature," or framework, for your sculpture from durable material. If you're using reinforcing rod or steel pipe, you may gain a few years in the losing battle against rust by coating the steel with epoxy paint. I'd bolt together an armature from pressure-treated 2″ lumber, painted with water-repellent preservative so that it doesn't absorb water (the resultant swelling could crack the sculpture). In either case, make the "legs" of the armature long enough to bury in the footing. For lighter parts of the sculpture, you can form an armature from galvanized hardware cloth (heavy screening with 1/4″ holes) filled with mortar.

3. Build out from a wooden armature by nailing hardware cloth to it with roofing nails or heavy staples.

4. Ladies and gentlemen! Mix your mortar.
   Caution: Wear rubber gloves and don't breathe the dust. And when you're cleaning up, don't dump the waste in the sink — the sand will plug the drain.
   Proportions:
   (All materials are available at hardware stores or masonry suppliers.)
   94 lb. Portland cement
   50 lb. mason's lime (not masonry cement)
   Eighteen rounded #3 shovelfuls of clean, dry mason's sand
   Start with a manageable amount of mortar, no more than a quarter batch. Weigh on a bathroom scale:
        23 1/2 lb. Portland cement, and
        12 1/2 lb. lime.
   Add 4 1/2 shovelfuls of sand.

Mix the materials dry, then add the minimum amount of water needed to blend the stone soup, and continue mixing for three minutes. As a reformed mason, I prefer mixing in a wheelbarrow, but Lisa reports that the new-fangled mortar mixing tubs that roll along the ground work quite well. Acrylic bonding agents will greatly strengthen the mortar.

5. Start filling in the sculpture with mortar. Use several applications — don't try to do everything in one step. Leave the surface rough so that the next application will adhere, and always cover the sculpture with burlap and plastic to keep the mortar moist while it sets — otherwise it will be weak. In dry weather, dampen the mortar periodically with a spray bottle.

6. When you get to the finish level, press your embellishments into the wet mortar. Again, cover the sculpture so that it dries slowly.

7. You can further decorate with exterior latex paint, used full strength, or diluted to make a wash. Wet the surface and sponge the paint onto the sculpture.

Kit Carson rides a bucking bronco at Concrete Park.

A Word on Using These Plans

The key thing about building for the backyard, aside from its inherent satisfaction, is that it liberates you from the biggest headache of construction — the accuracy compulsion. In the backyard, $1/64''$ does not matter — in fact, depending on your disposition, $1/8''$ may not make much difference, either. So if a project does not come out exactly like the plans, don't worry too much. Your guests won't notice, and neither will your tomatoes.

If you're a newcomer to building, it's time to learn that the actual size of lumber does not equal its "nominal size" (except with plywood and other sheet materials).

- Width: 1×4s and 1×6s are actually $1/2''$ narrower than the nominal width; 1×8s and wider are $3/4''$ narrower than nominal width. Thus a 1×6 is $5 1/2''$ wide, and a 1×8 is $7 1/4''$ wide.

- Thickness: Most nominal $1''$ boards are $3/4''$ thick, but nominal $2''$ boards are $1 1/2''$ thick.

- **Important:** The attractive and rot-resistant #3 red cedar used in most wood projects in this book is sold in either $3/4''$ or $7/8''$ thickness, both nominally called one-inch material. Before starting one of these projects, search the lumber yards for the $7/8''$ variety that we've used. If you must use $3/4''$ material, adjust the plan dimensions accordingly.

- Dimensions in this book with the inch ($''$) symbol are actual dimensions — so a $2'' \times 2''$ is really that size. Dimensions without the inch symbol (for example, 2×2) are nominal sizes.

I've calculated the wood requirements on the stingy side. If you make mistakes (don't be ashamed — we all do), then you probably won't have enough wood. It may be best to buy extra wood; at worst, you'll have some for the next project.

OTHER HINTS

Most of these wood projects are fastened with rustproof deck screws, which are stronger, more accurate, and easier to use than nails. It's definitely best to drill a hole before screwing, as cedar splits easily. I also suggest countersinking the holes to hide the screw heads. If you're planning to use a variable-speed drill to drill and drive the screws, a combination drill-countersink bit is extremely handy.

It's a good idea to predrill nail holes (especially on small pieces or near an end) to prevent splitting. Speaking of nails, if you're not familiar with the archaic but lovely designation for nail sizes in the United States, recognize that a lower-case "d" indicates "penny." Generally, we'll use galvanized box or (better) galvanzed siding nails.

Although it's not mentioned in every wood project, cedar and pressure-treated wood both appreciate protection from water and the ultraviolet portion of sunlight. Thus, exterior stain or water-repellent preservative will extend the life span of your creations.

Likewise, I haven't always mentioned sandpapering, but most projects greatly benefit from a quick papering with medium and then fine paper, which smoothes the wood and removes splinters. It's best to do this dull, dusty, but necessary chore after you cut the parts, but before assembly.

GLOSSARY

Batten. A thin strip of wood used to seal a joint or hold material beneath it.

Bevel. A cut that is not at 90° (not square) to the surface of the wood.

Butt joint. A simple, weak joint where square board ends meet without angles, rabbets, or other fanciness.

Circular saw. An electric saw with a circular blade, for cutting dimension lumber (for example, 2 × 4s) and plywood.

Countersink. A depression shaped like an inverted cone, allowing a screw head to sit flush to the surface or below it.

Coping saw. A hand saw shaped like the Big Dipper (but somewhat smaller) used to cut curves.

Crosscut. To cut at right angles to the grain.

Crosscut saw. A hand saw with small teeth made to cut across the grain.

Dado. A rectangular groove removed from a board, usually to hold another board in a dado joint. Also the thick saw blade that cuts a dado (for a table saw only).

Hacksaw. A hand saw specially made to cut metal.

Hand saw. Various types of muscle-powered saws.

Jigsaw. A floor-mounted power saw with a continuous looping blade, used to cut curves.

Kerf. The narrow section of wood, usually about $\frac{1}{8}''$ wide, removed by a saw.

Lag screw. A heavy-duty wood screw with a hexagonal or square head, driven with a wrench.

Miter. To cut a board at a nonsquare angle but at 90° to the surface.

Polebarn nail. A long thick nail with rings on its shank, for heavy-duty fastening.

Rabbet. A square section removed from the edge or end of a board.

Rasp. A tool resembling a coarse file, used to quickly remove wood.

Rip. To saw wood parallel to the grain.

Rip saw. A hand saw with large teeth, made to cut parallel to the grain.

Ripping. A narrow strip of wood ripped from a larger one.

Router. An electric tool that somewhat resembles a drill, made to shape the edges or faces of lumber. Routers can cut many shapes, depending on the bit selected.

Saber saw. A small power tool with a short, straight, reciprocating blade, made to cut curves.

Screed. A board that levels concrete or sand when it is slid back and forth. The screed rests on form boards at both ends.

Shim. A thin piece of wood used to correct deviations in angle or length.

Table saw. A floor-mounted power saw with a circular blade that pokes through a flat table.

PHOTO CREDITS

Cathy Wilkinson Barash: 55

Gay Bumgarner/Photo/Nats: 44

Karen Bussolini: 105

Derek Fell: iii, 1, 11, 25, 26, 57, 70, 80

Mary Nemeth/Photo/Nats: 16

David Tenenbaum: 86, 106, 107, 108, 109 top, 109 bottom, 112

INDEX

Page numbers in italics refer to illustrations.

Titles available in the Taylor's Weekend Gardening Guides series:

Organic Pest and Disease Control	$12.95
Safe and Easy Lawn Care	12.95
Window Boxes	12.95
Attracting Birds and Butterflies	12.95
Water Gardens	12.95
Easy, Practical Pruning	12.95
The Winter Garden	12.95
Backyard Building Projects	12.95
Indoor Gardens	12.95
Plants for Problem Places	12.95

At your bookstore or by calling 1-800-225-3362

Prices subject to change without notice

4339